RECORDED VERSIONS
GUITAR

AUTHENTIC TRANSCRIPTIONS
WITH NOTES AND TABLATURE

AVENGED SEVENF...

HAIL to the KING

MW00824401

Music transcriptions by Pete Billmann, Aurelien Budynek, Jeff Jacobson, and David Stocker

ISBN 978-1-4803-6113-3

HAL•LEONARD®
CORPORATION

7777 W. BLUEMOUND RD. P.O. BOX 13819 MILWAUKEE, WI 53213

In Australia Contact:
Hal Leonard Australia Pty. Ltd.
4 Lentara Court
Cheltenham, Victoria, 3192 Australia
Email: ausadmin@halleonard.com.au

Visit Hal Leonard Online at
www.halleonard.com

Shepherd of Fire

Words and Music by Matthew Sanders, Jonathan Seward, Brian Haner, Jr. and Zachary Baker

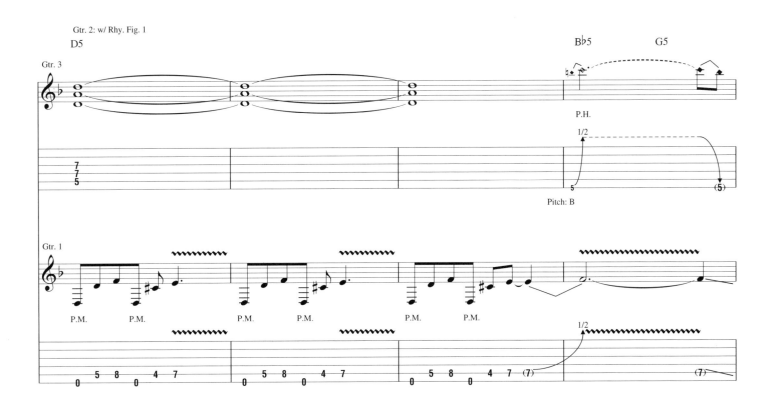

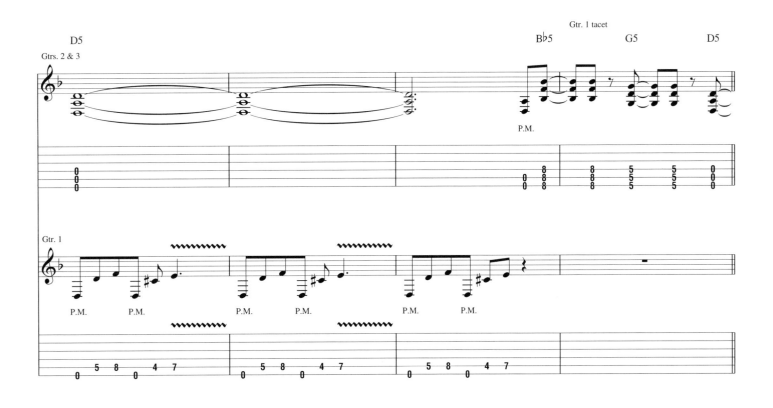

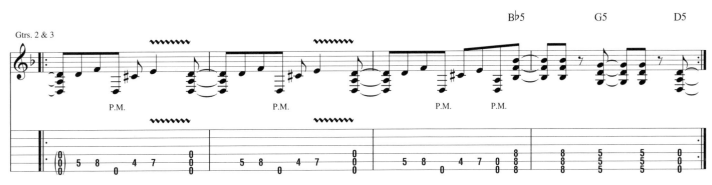

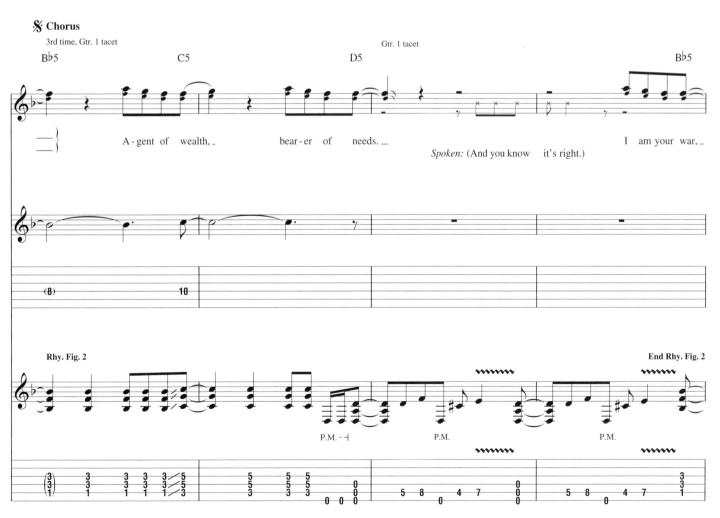

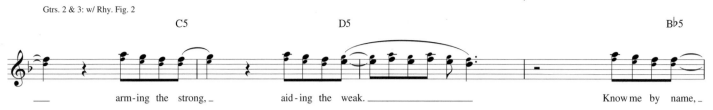

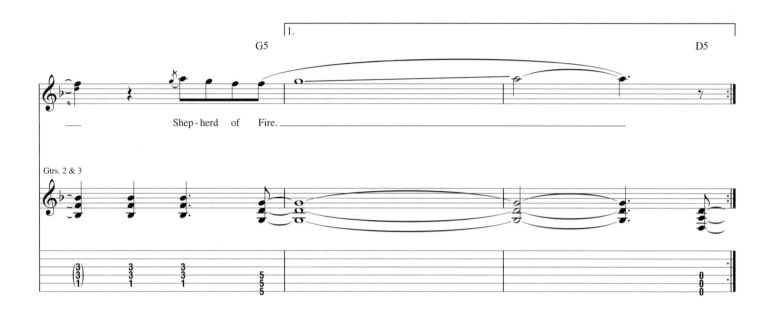

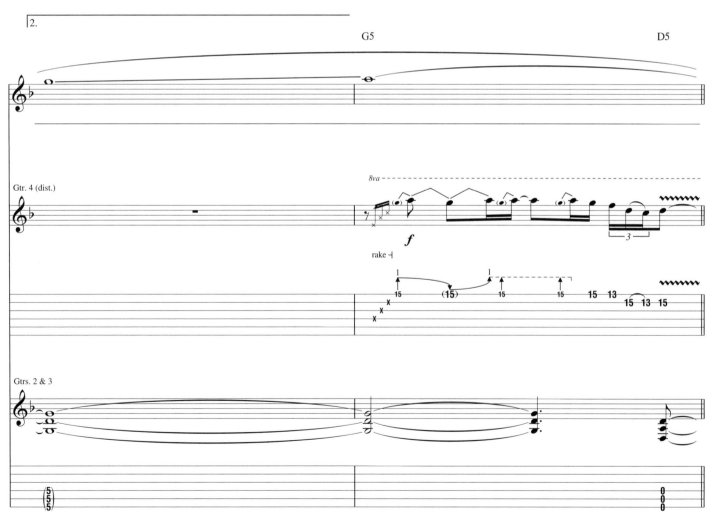

Guitar Solo

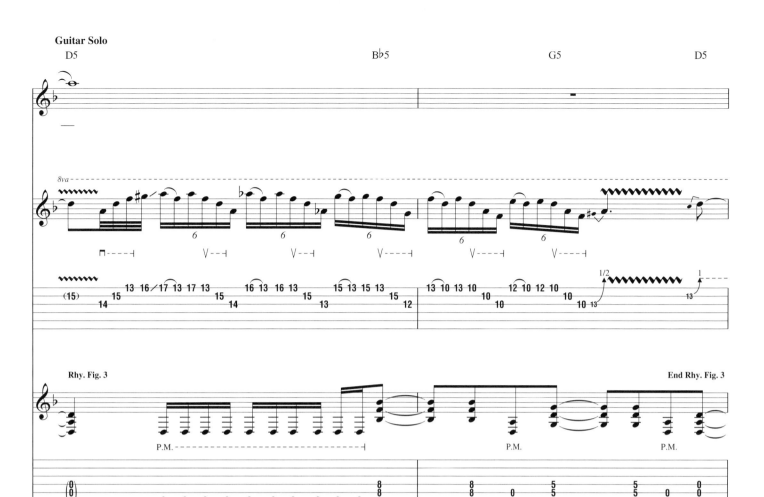

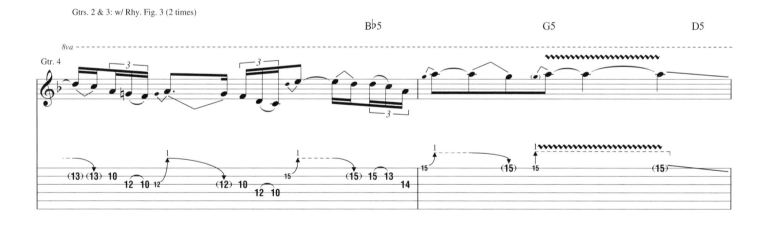

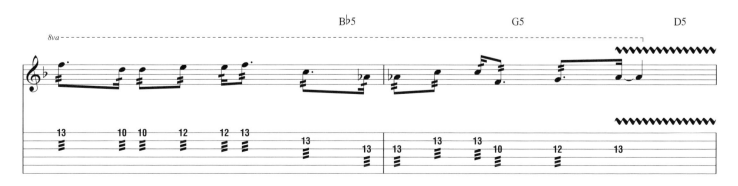

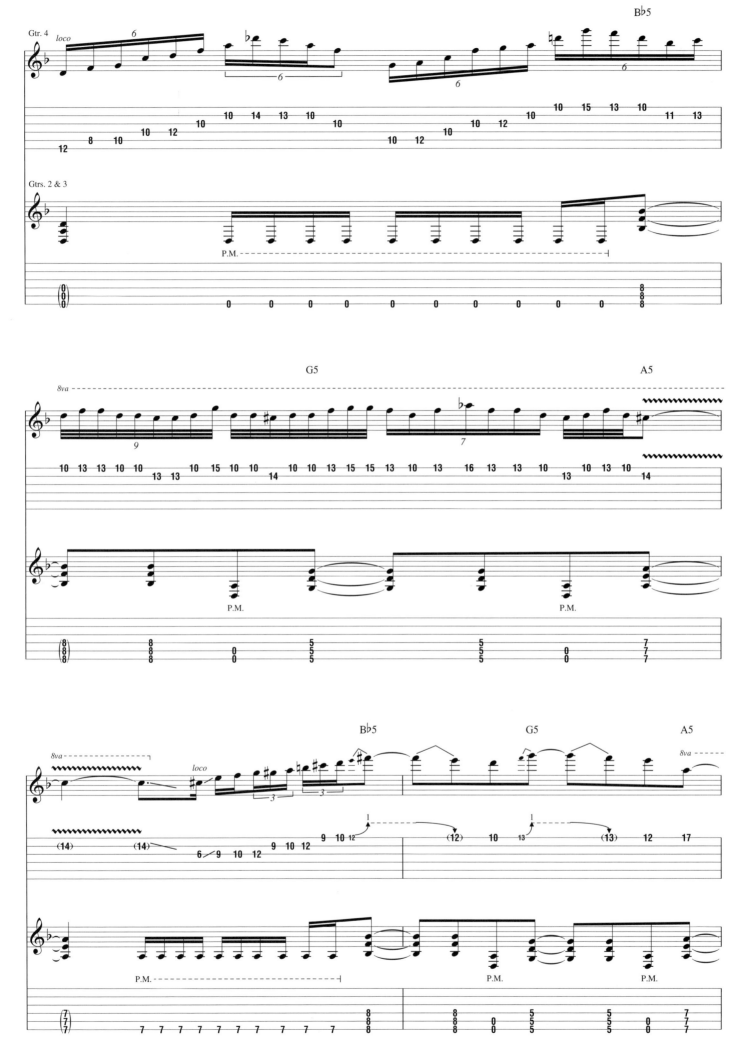

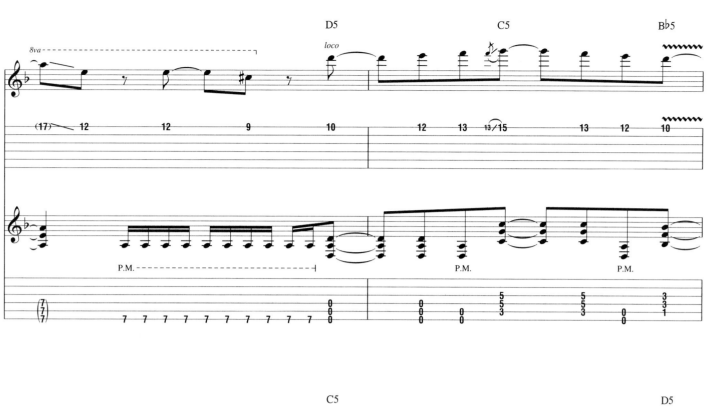

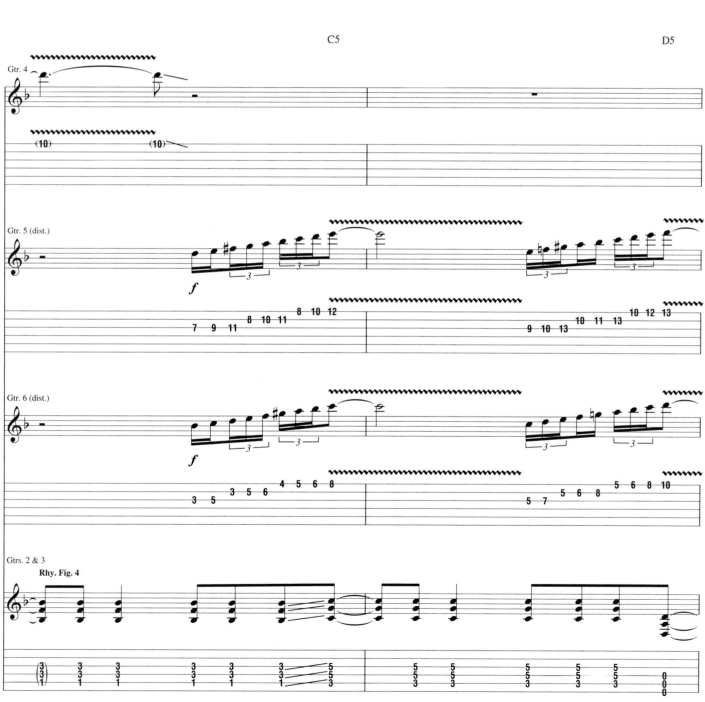

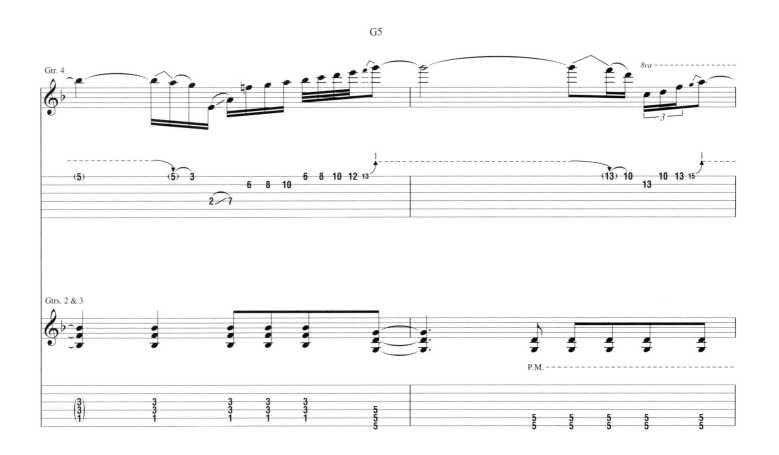

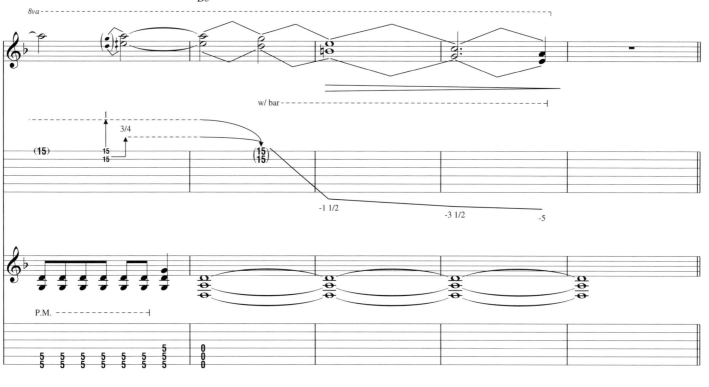

Bridge

Gtr. 1: w/ Riff A (1st 2 meas., 4 times)
Gtrs. 2 & 3 tacet

Spoken: Disciple of the cross and champion in suffering, immerse yourself into the kingdom of redemption.

Pardon your mind through the chains of the divine. Make way the Shepherd of Fire.

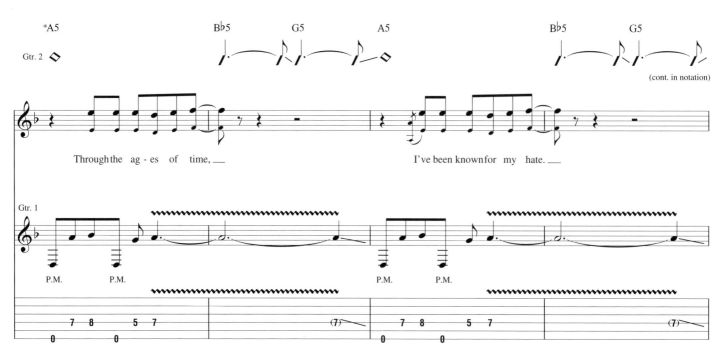

Through the ag - es of time, ___ I've been known for my hate. ___

*See top of first page of song for chord diagrams pertaining to rhythm slashes.

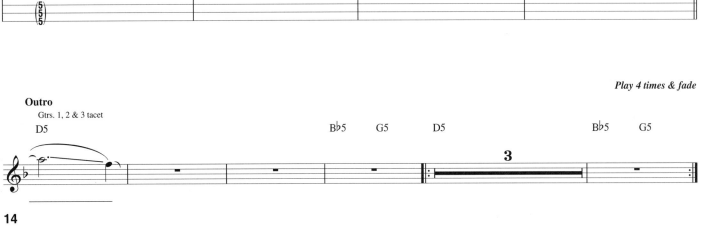

Hail to the King

Words and Music by Matthew Sanders, Jonathan Seward, Brian Haner, Jr. and Zachary Baker

Drop D tuning, down 1/2 step:
(low to high) Db-Ab-Db-Gb-Bb-Eb

Intro
Moderately ♩ = 118

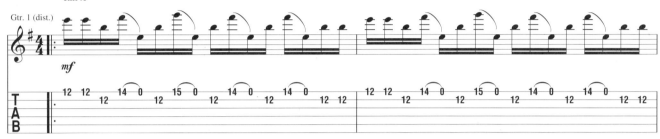

*Chord symbols reflect implied harmony.

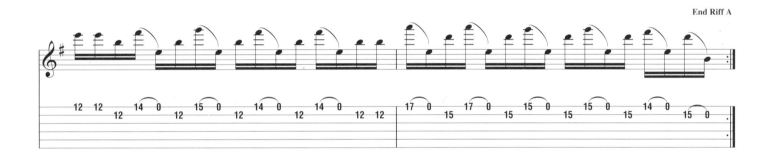

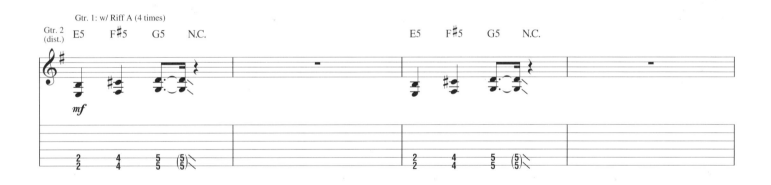

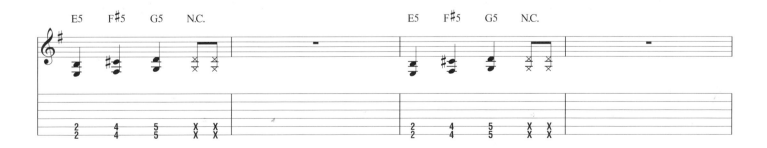

Roy - al flames will carve a path in cha - os, _____
Let the wat - er flow with shades of red, _____ now. _____

Gtr. 1: w/ Riff C
Gtrs. 2 & 3: w/ Rhy. Fig. 4

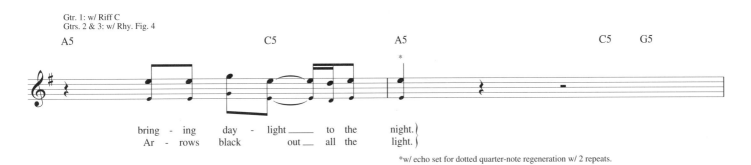

bring - ing day - light _____ to the night.
Ar - rows black out _____ all the light.

*w/ echo set for dotted quarter-note regeneration w/ 2 repeats.

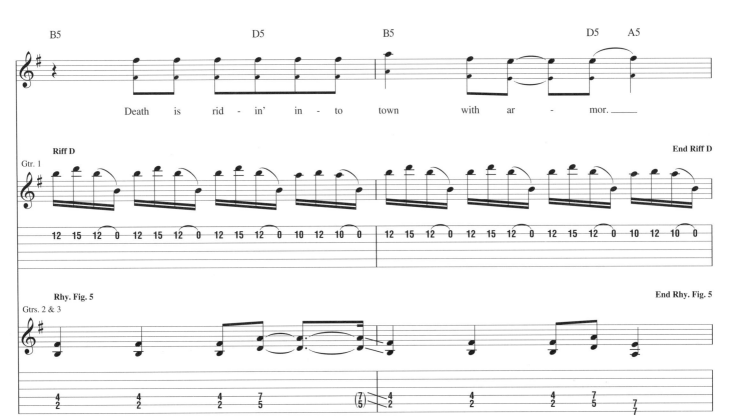

Death is rid - in' in - to town with ar - mor. _____

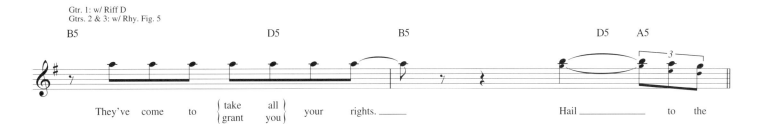

They've come to {take all / grant you} your rights. _____ Hail _____ to the

Chorus

king, hail to the

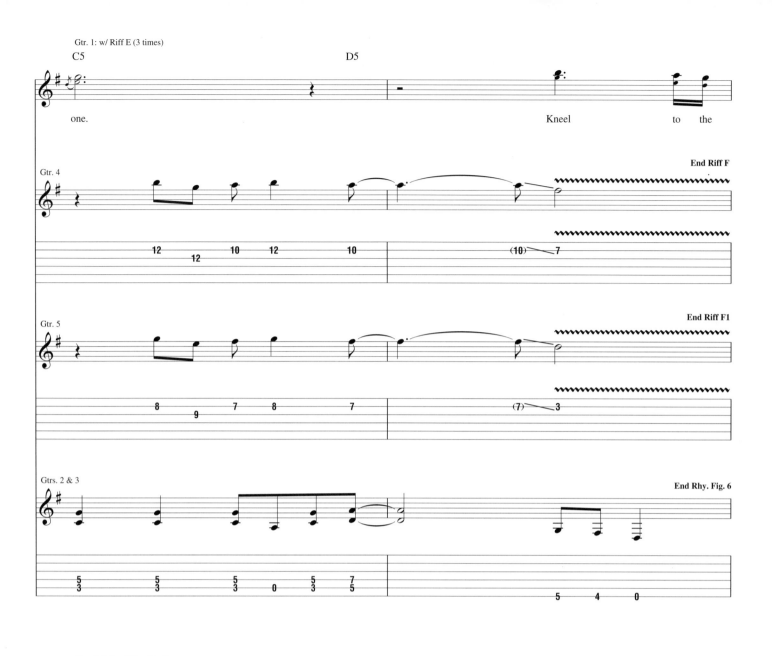

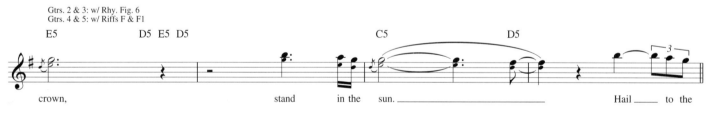

Interlude

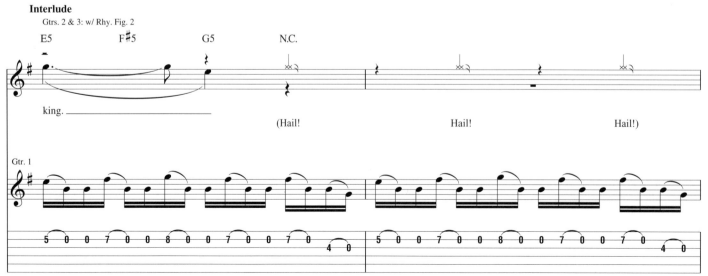

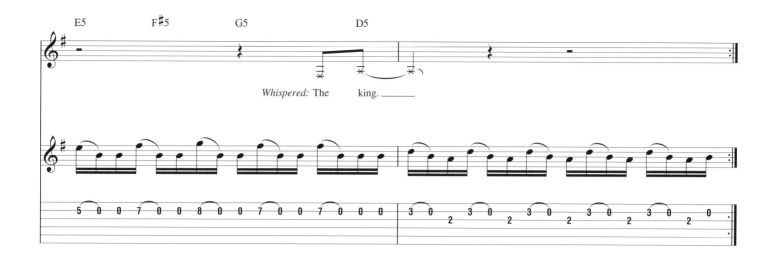

Guitar Solo

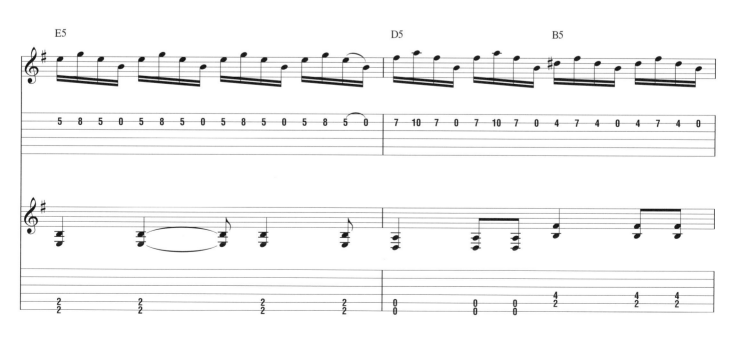

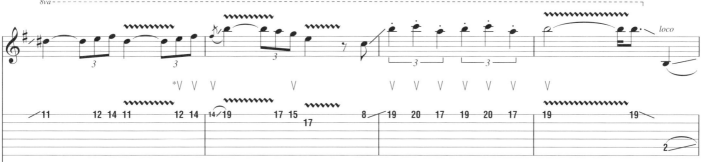

*Press edge of pick into string and pull upwards (upstroke), then immediately
preceding next note, repeat process, producing harmonic effect between notes.

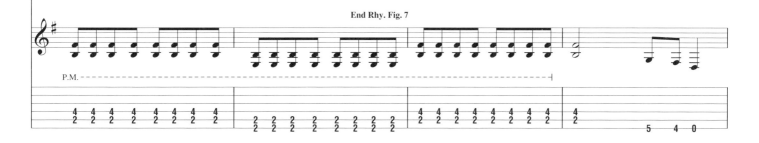

Gtrs. 2 & 3: w/ Rhy. Fig. 7

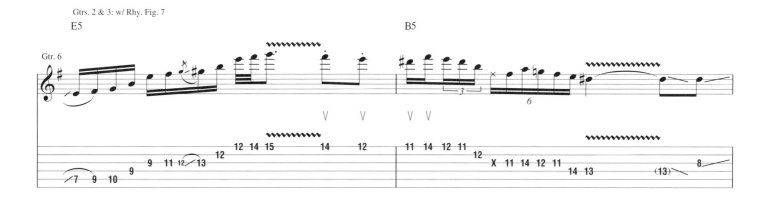

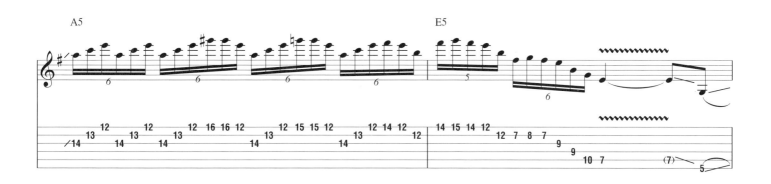

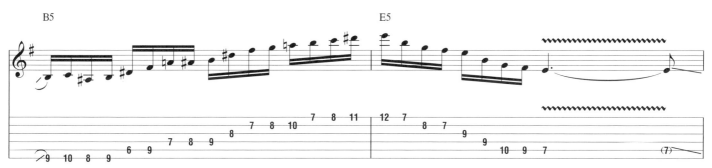

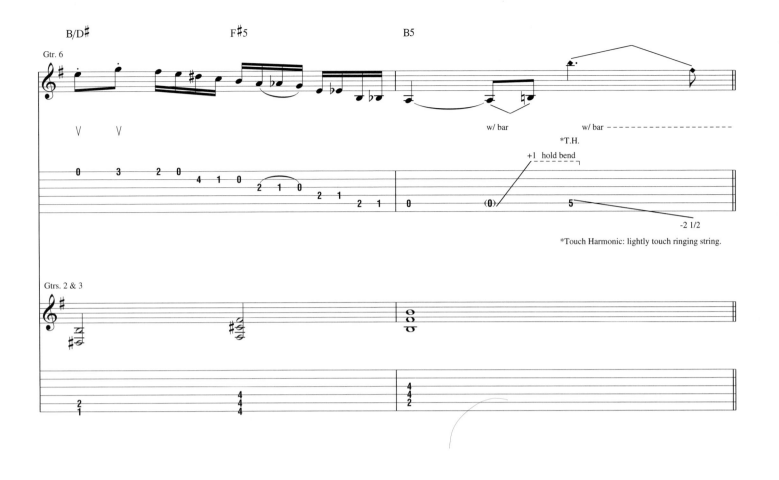

Interlude

Gtr. 1: w/ Riff A

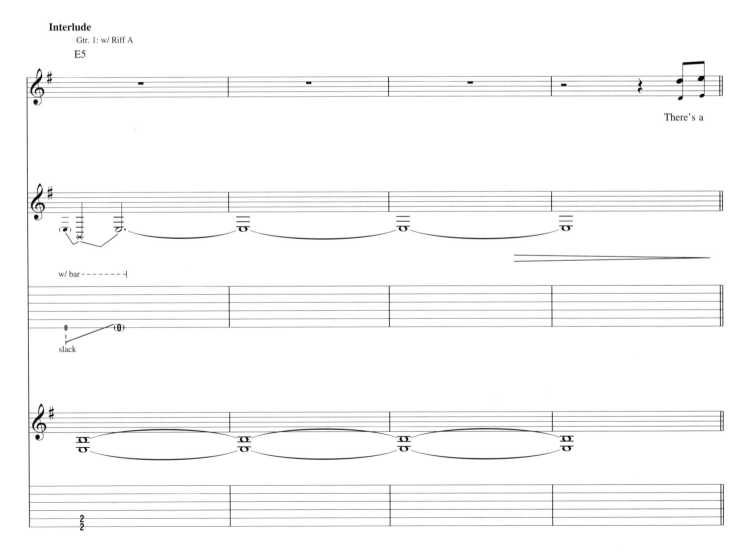

Bridge

Gtr. 1: w/ Riff A (1 1/2 times)
Gtrs. 2 & 3: w/ Rhy. Fig. 1 (1 1/2 times)
Gtr. 6 tacet

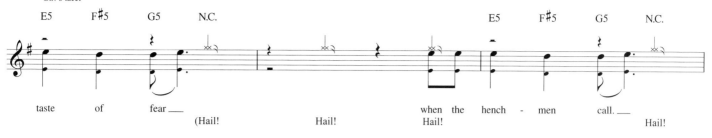

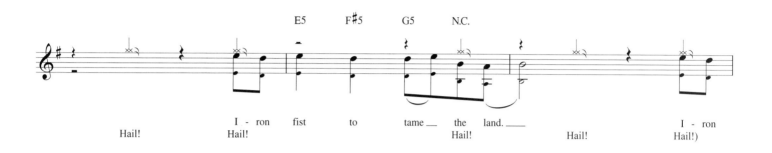

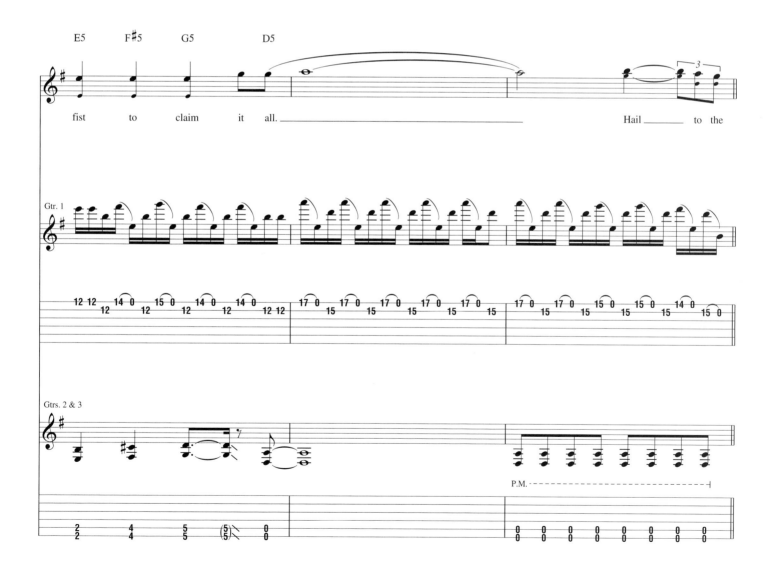

Chorus

Gtr. 1: w/ Riff E (8 times)
Gtrs. 2 & 3: w/ Rhy. Fig. 6 (4 times)
Gtrs. 4 & 5: w/ Riffs F & F1 (4 times)

king,   hail to the one.   Kneel to the crown,

stand in the sun. _____ Hail ___ to the sun. _____ Hail ___ to the

Outro

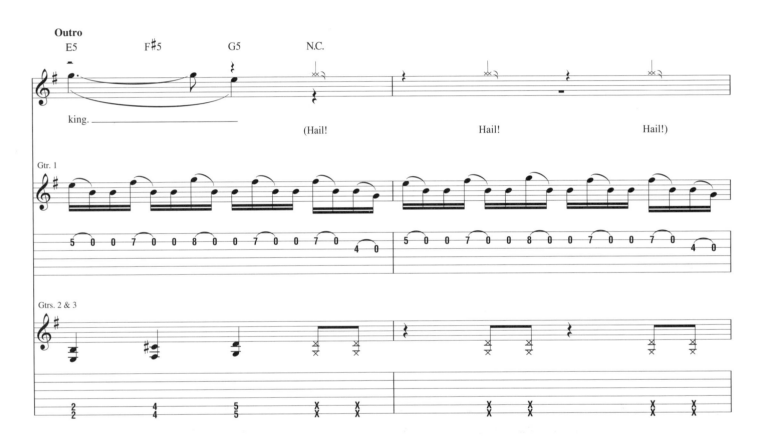

king. _____

(Hail!)   Hail!   Hail!)

Gtr. 1

Gtrs. 2 & 3

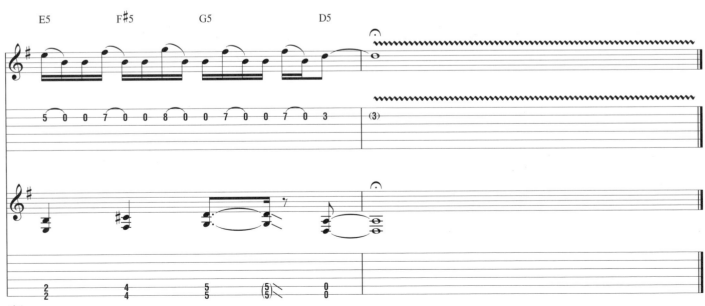

Doing Time

Words and Music by Matthew Sanders, Jonathan Seward, Brian Haner, Jr. and Zachary Baker

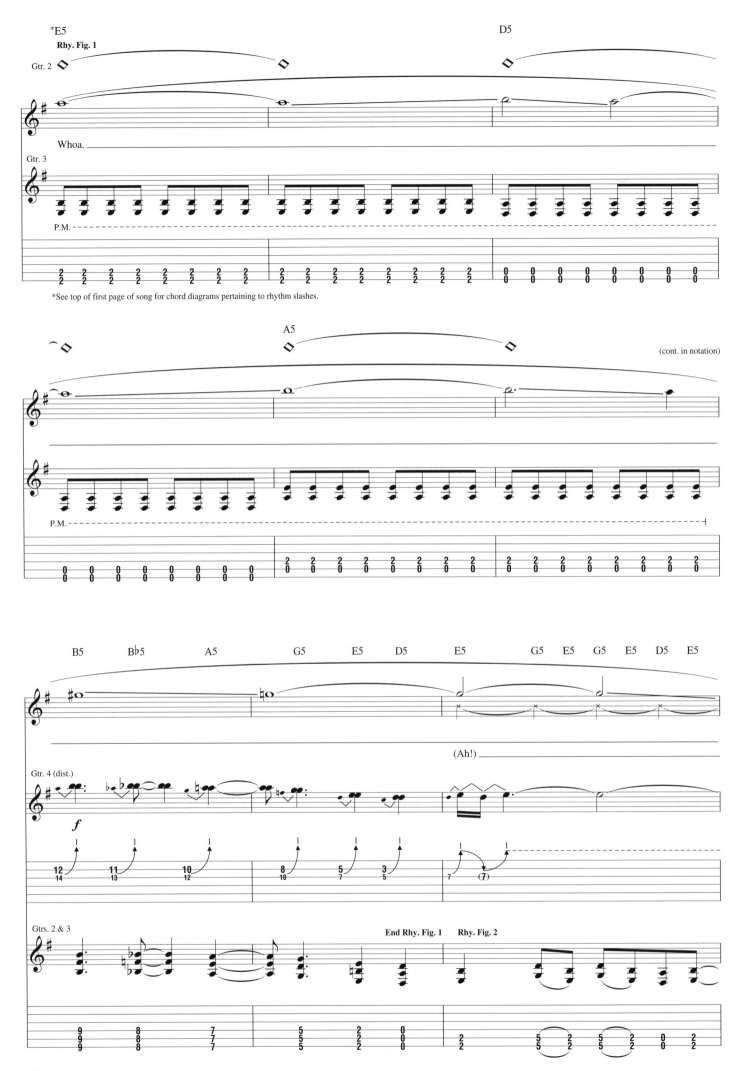

*See top of first page of song for chord diagrams pertaining to rhythm slashes.

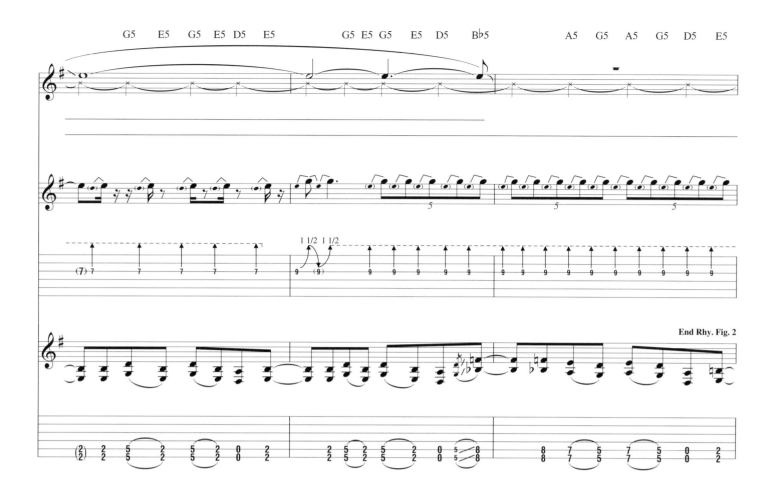

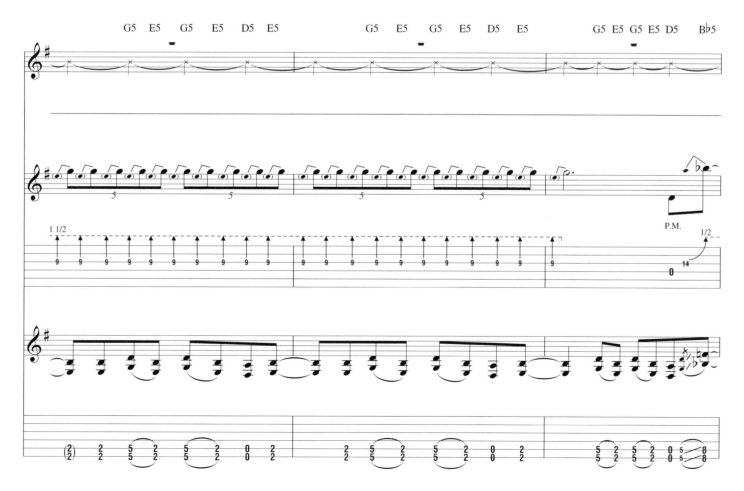

Verse

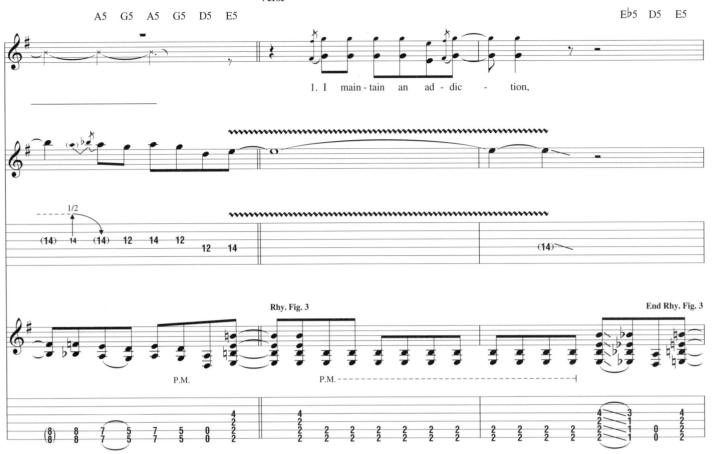

1. I main - tain an ad - dic - tion,

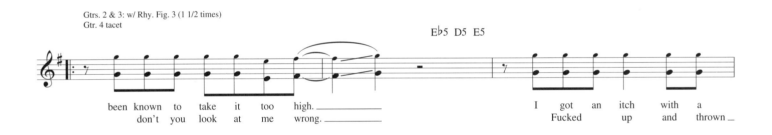

been known to take it too high. ____
don't you look at me wrong. ____

I got an itch with a
Fucked up and thrown ____

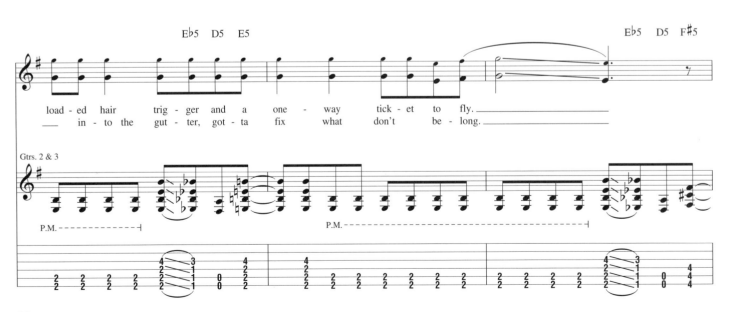

load - ed hair trig - ger and a one - way tick - et to fly. ____
____ in - to the gut - ter, got - ta fix what don't be - long. ____

Guitar Solo

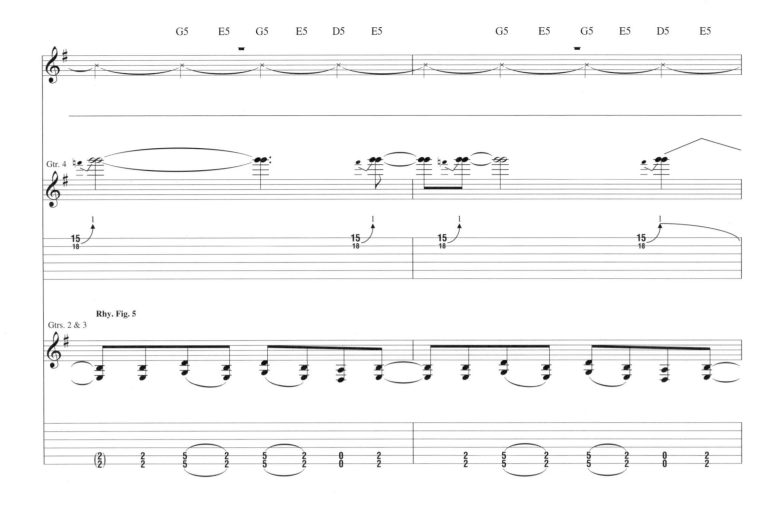

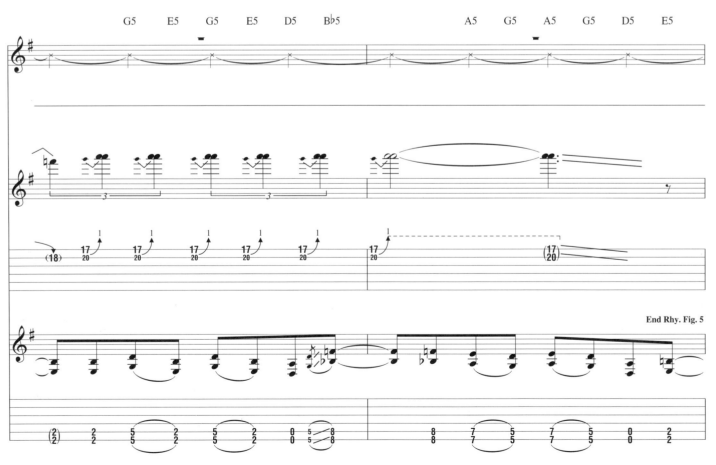

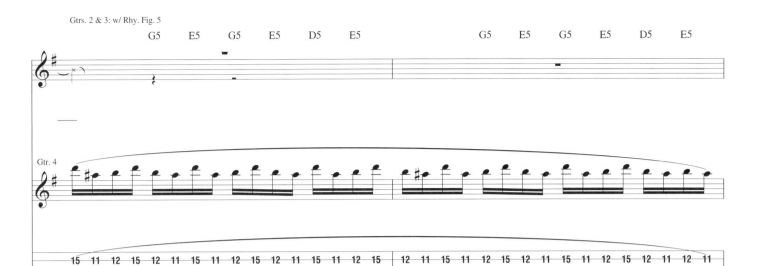

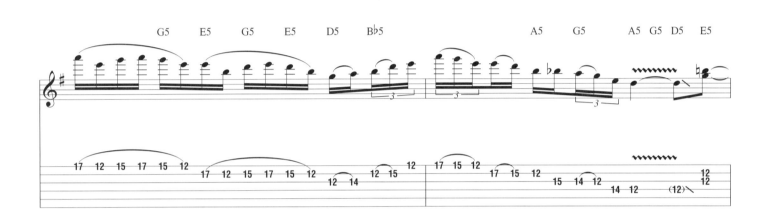

Interlude

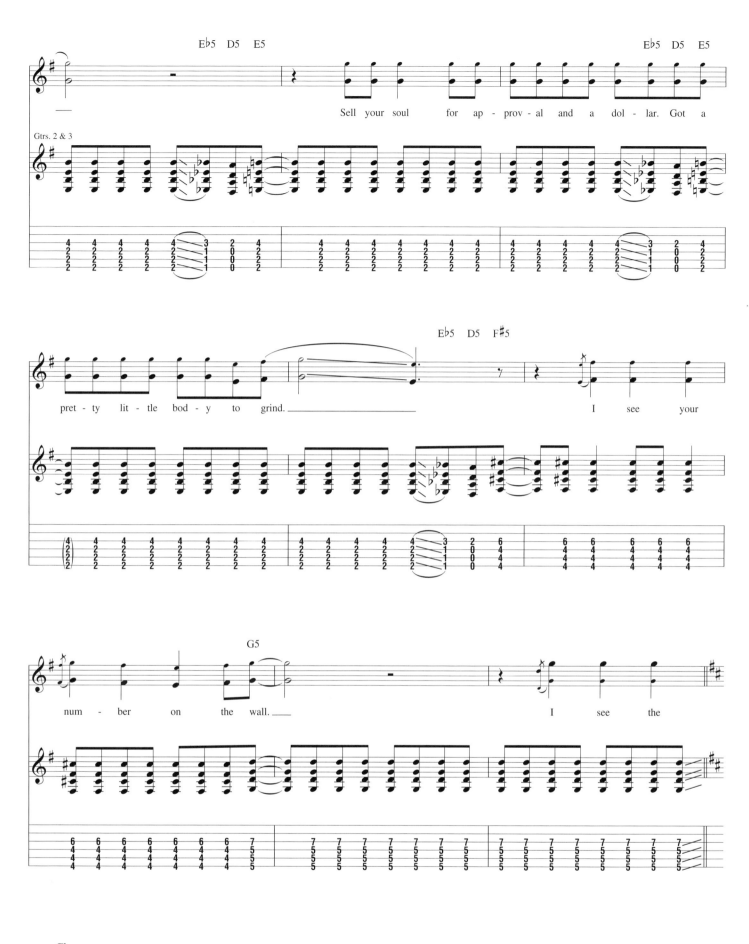

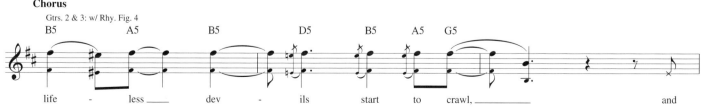

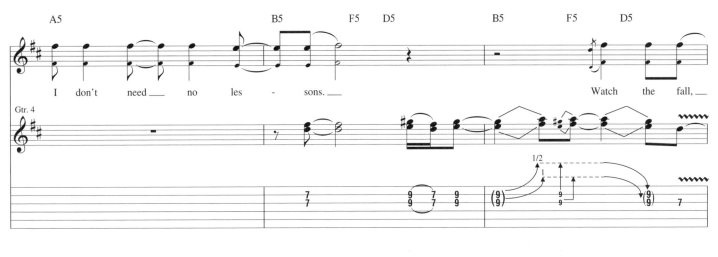

I don't need ___ no les - sons. ___ Watch the fall, ___

Gtr. 4

Gtrs. 2 & 3: w/ Rhy. Fig. 4 (last 4 meas.)

___ you lost my ___ at - ten - tion.

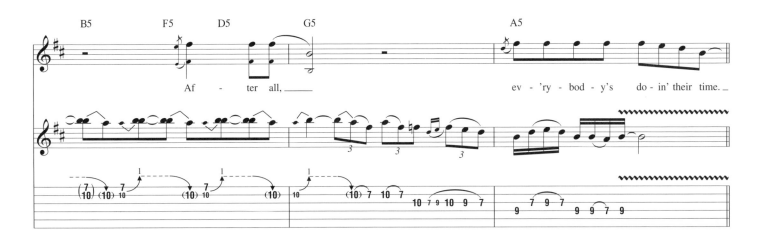

Af - ter all, ___ ev - 'ry - bod - y's do - in' their time. ___

Outro

Gtrs. 2 & 3

___ Time. ___

Gtr. 4

This Means War

Words and Music by Matthew Sanders, Jonathan Seward, Brian Haner, Jr. and Zachary Baker

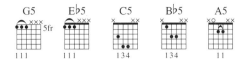

Drop D tuning:
(low to high) D-A-D-G-B-E

*Chord symbols reflect basic harmony.

1. Hide my face a - gain, __ har - bor in the shad - ows. __
2. Lash your tongue of bane, __ car - ry me to no - where. __
3. Walk the ra - zor's edge, __ cut in - to the mad - ness. __

Interlude

D.S. al Coda 1
(skip repeat)

⊕ Coda 1

Chorus

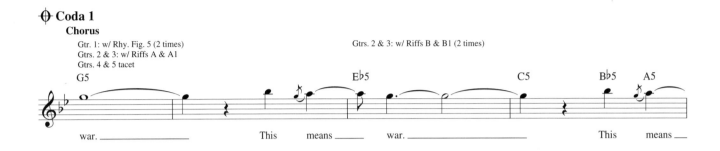

Guitar Solo

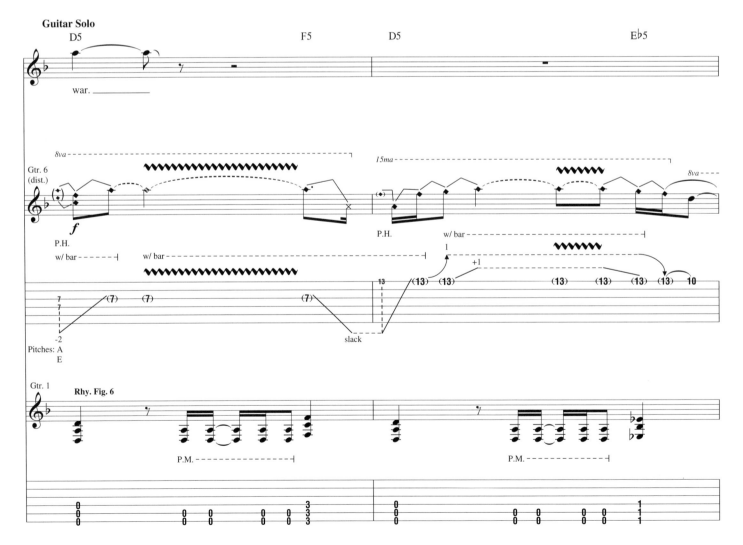

44

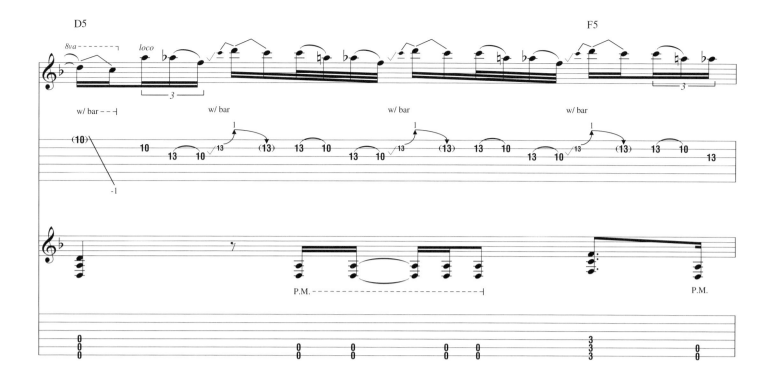

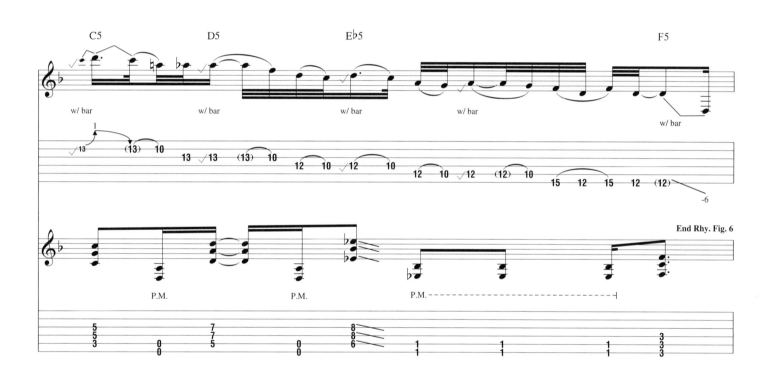

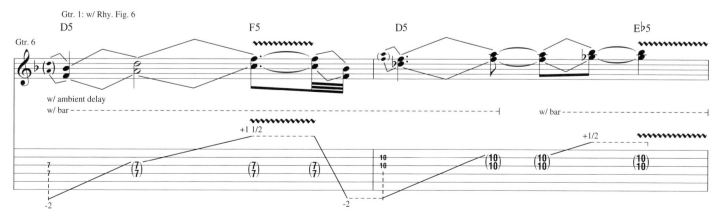

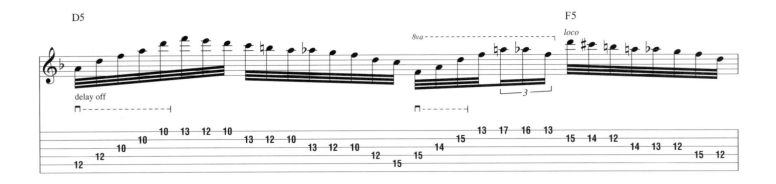

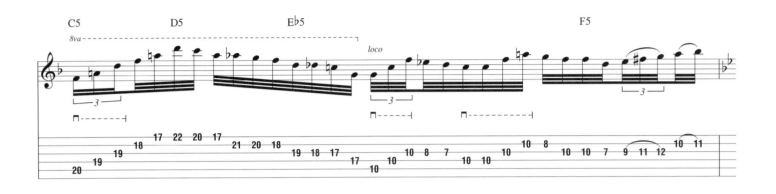

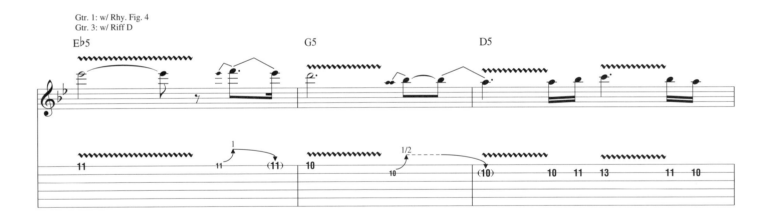

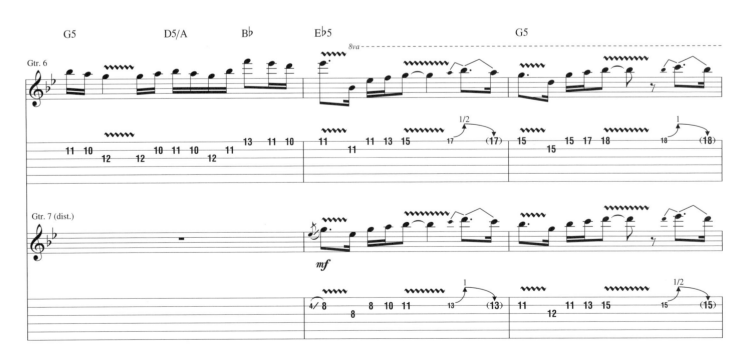

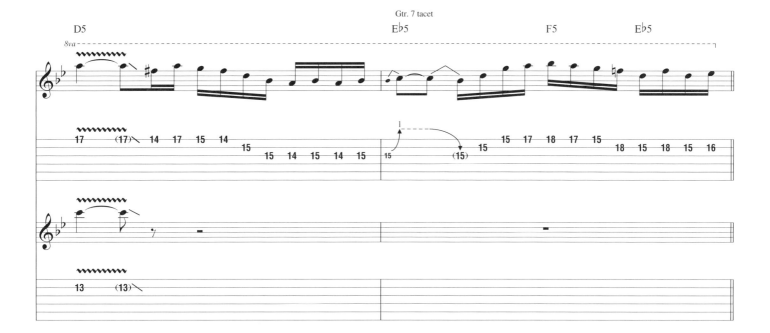

Bridge

Gtr. 1: w/ Rhy. Fig. 1
Gtrs. 2 & 3: w/ Riffs A & A1

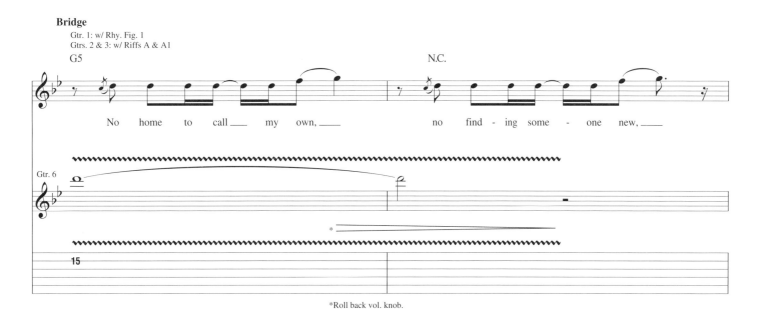

No home to call ___ my own, ___ no find-ing some - one new, ___

*Roll back vol. knob.

Gtrs. 2 & 3: w/ Riffs B & B1 (2 times)

no one to break ___ the fall, ___ no one to see ___ me through. ___

No name to car - ry on, ___ no prom - ise for ___ to - day, ___

Gtrs. 2 & 3: w/ Riffs C & C1

no one to hear ___ the call, ___ no tat - tered flag ___ to raise.

Requiem

Words and Music by Matthew Sanders, Jonathan Seward, Brian Haner, Jr. and Zachary Baker

Drop D tuning, down 1/2 step:
(low to high) Db-Ab-Db-Gb-Bb-Eb

Intro
Moderately fast ♩ = 142

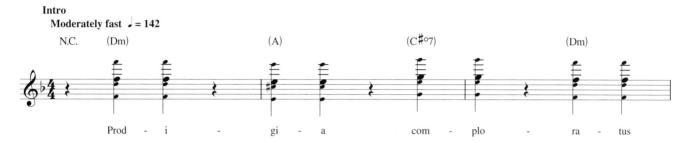

Prod - i - gi - a com - plo - ra - tus

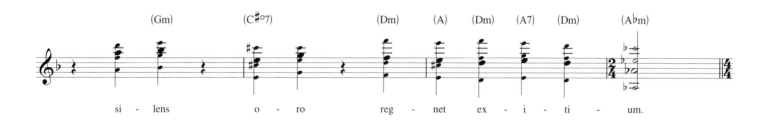

si - lens o - ro reg - net ex - i - ti - um.

*Chord symbols reflect combined harmony.

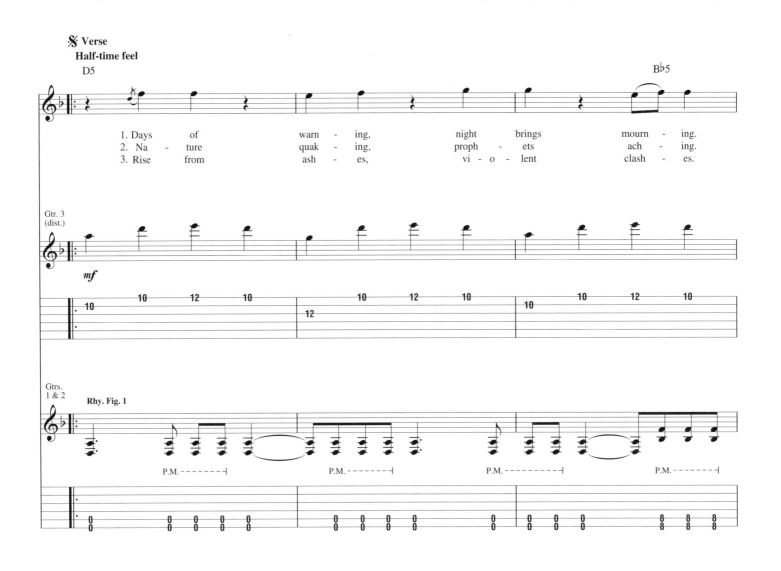

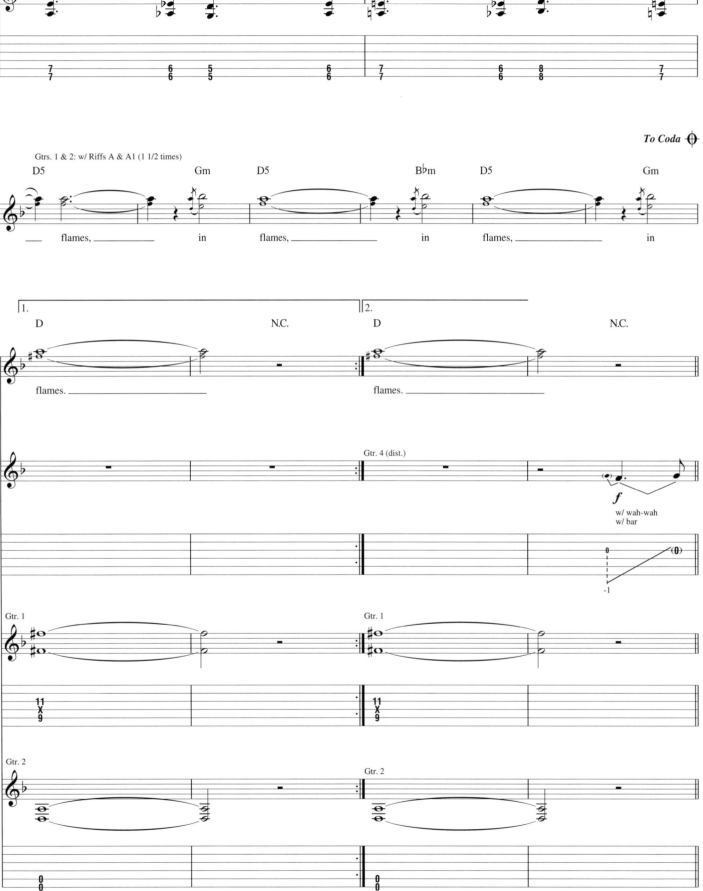

Guitar Solo

Gtrs. 1 & 2: w/ Rhy. Fig. 1 (2 times)

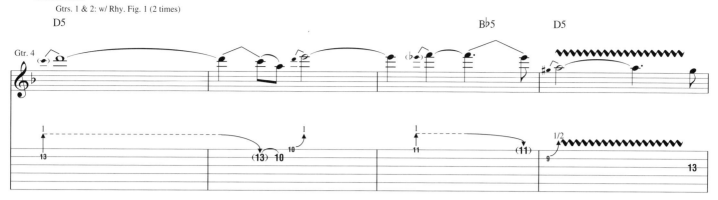

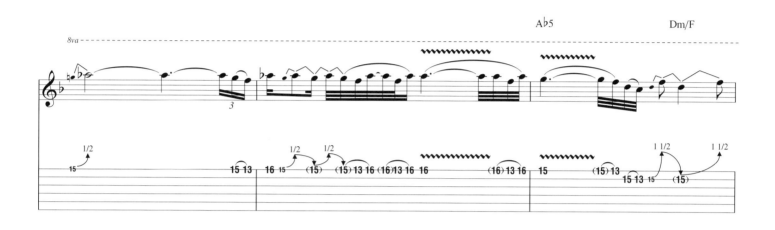

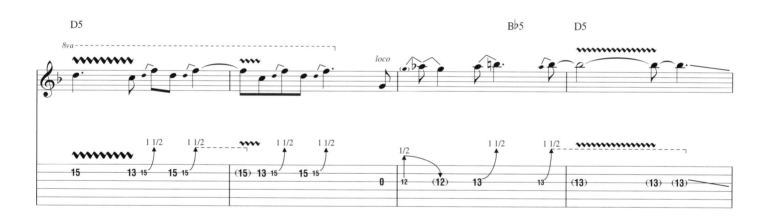

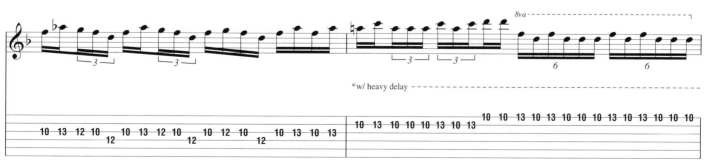

*Delay set for quarter-note regeneration w/ 5 repeats.

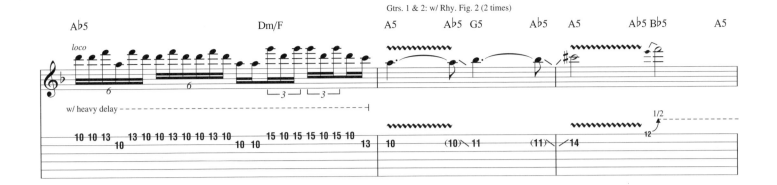

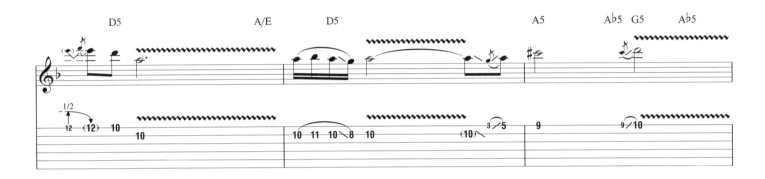

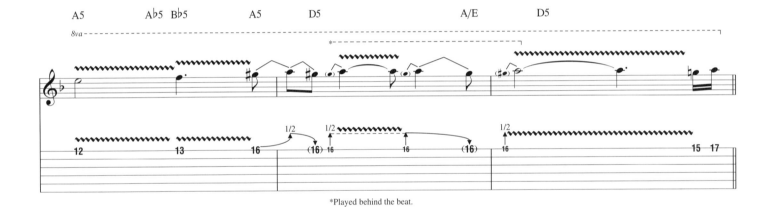

*Played behind the beat.

Bridge

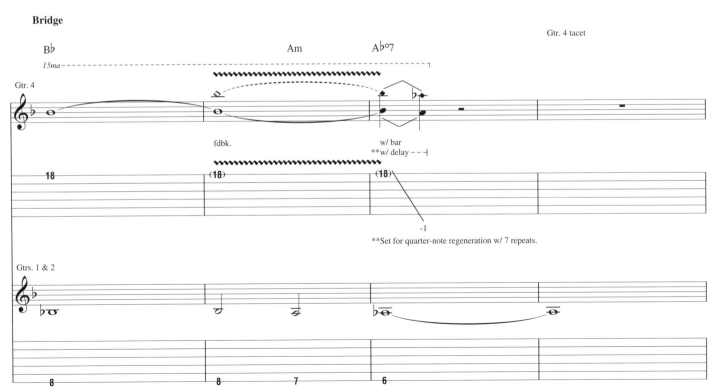

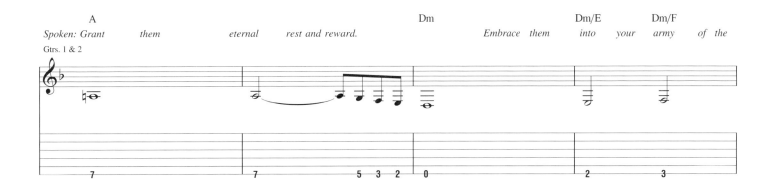

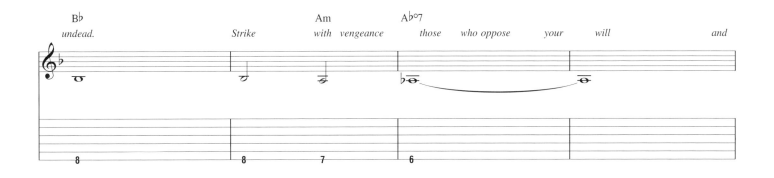

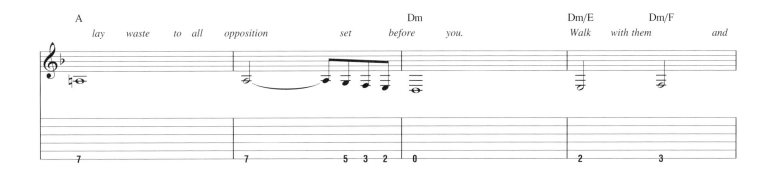

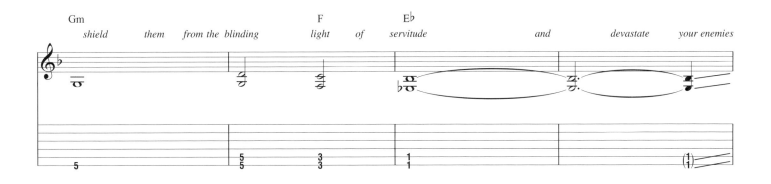

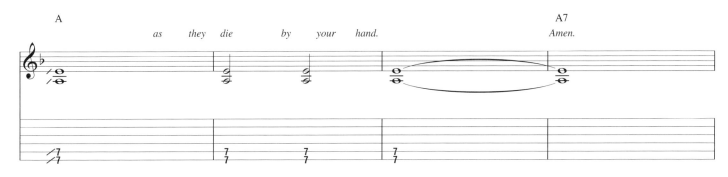

Coda

D.S. al Coda

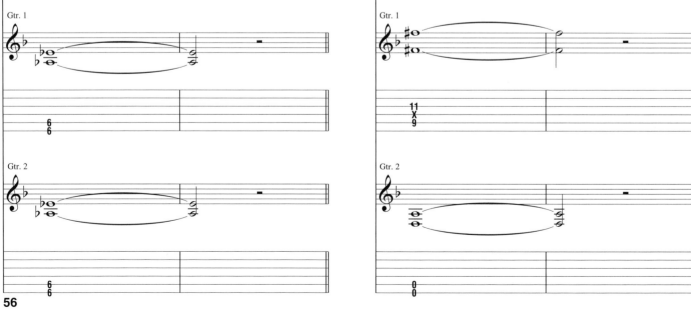

Crimson Day

Words and Music by Matthew Sanders, Jonathan Seward, Brian Haner, Jr. and Zachary Baker

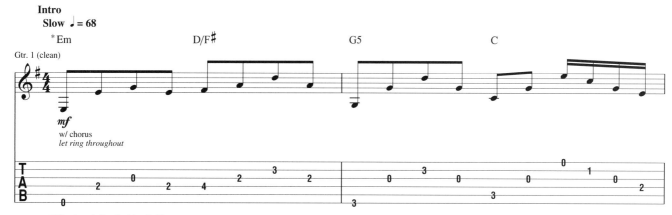

*Chord symbols reflect implied harmony.

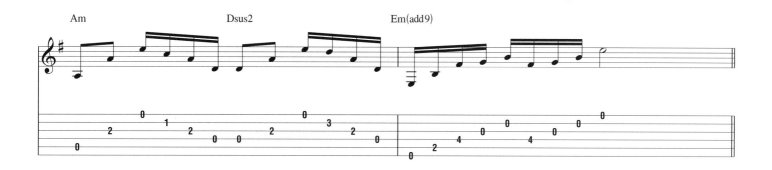

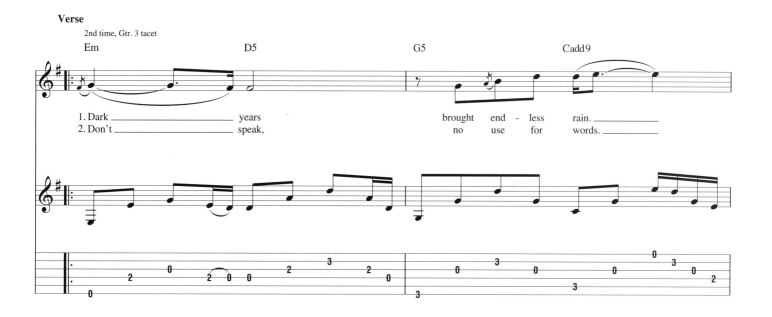

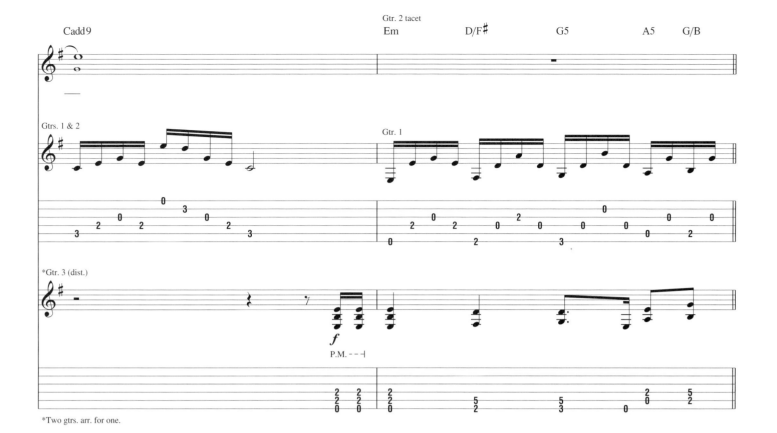

*Two gtrs. arr. for one.

𝄋 Chorus

3rd time, Gtr. 4: w/ Fill 1

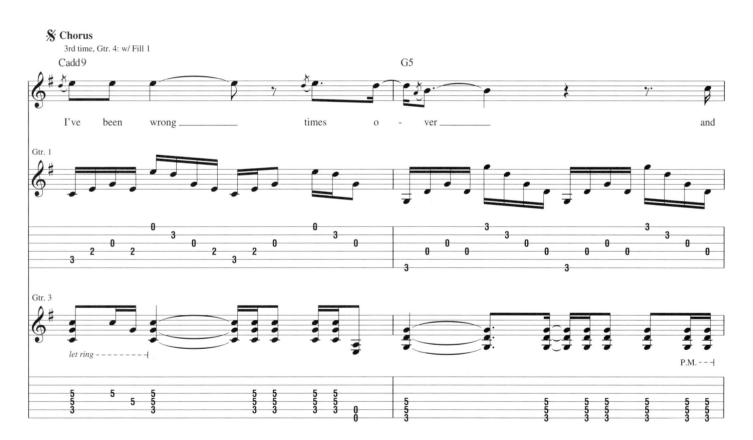

I've been wrong _____ times o - ver _____ and

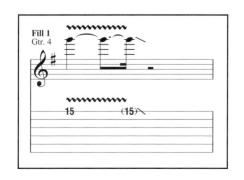

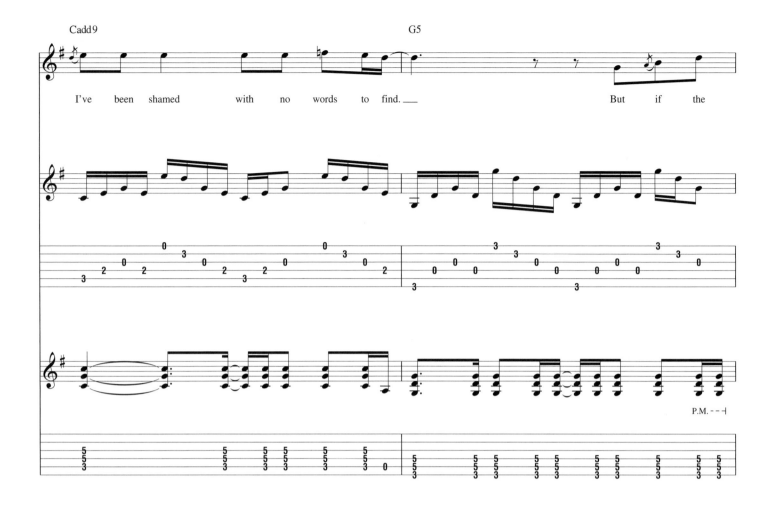

I've been shamed with no words to find. ___ But if the

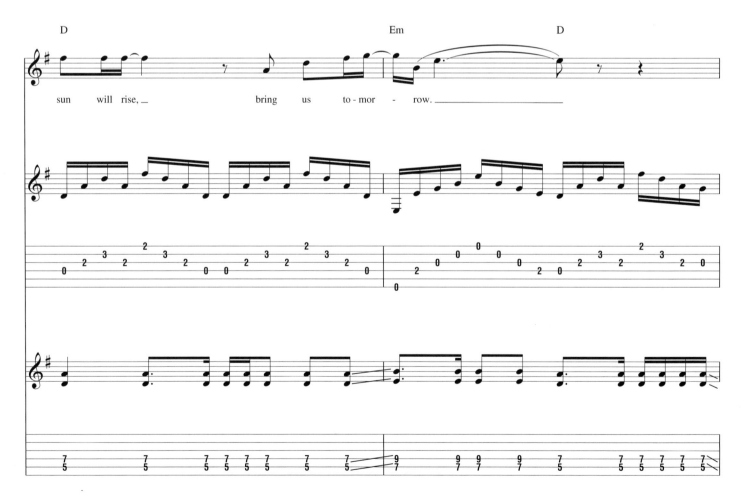

sun will rise, __ bring us to - mor - row. _____

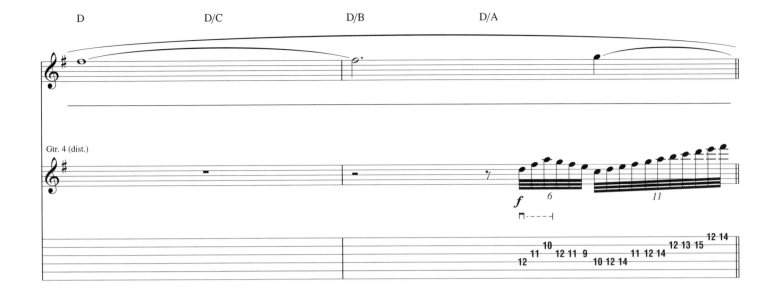

Guitar Solo

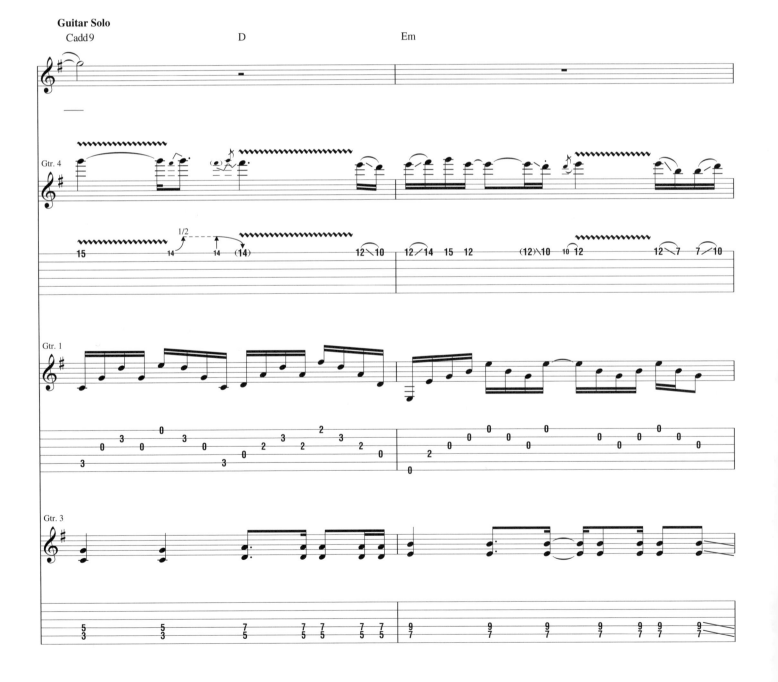

Cadd9   D   Em   D5   Cadd9   G/B

65

Gtr. 5 tacet
Am
D
Em
Gtr. 4
hold bend
Gtr. 1
Gtr. 3
P.M.
Bridge
Gtr. 1: w/ Riff A (1st 2 meas.)
Gtrs. 3 & 4 tacet
Am
Em
I've come so far to meet you here, to
D
Cadd9
share this life with one I hold so dear.
Gtr. 1
Gtr. 1: w/ Riff A
Am
Em
And I won't speak but what is true. The

world out - side_____ cre - at - ed just_____ for you,_____ it's for you, __

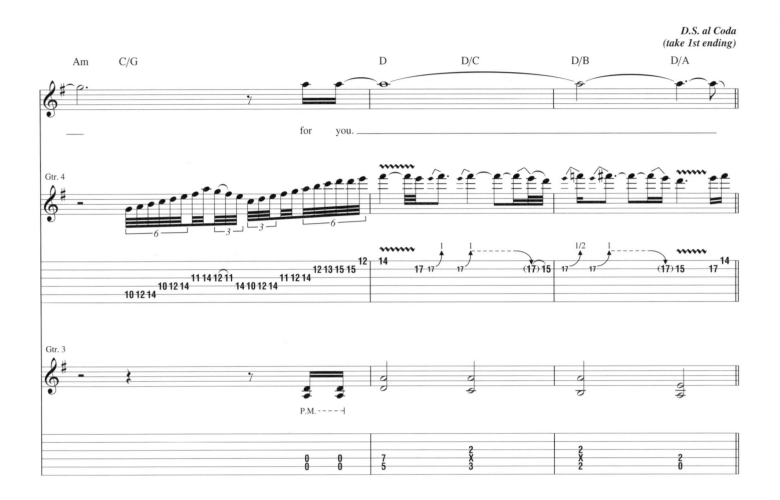

D.S. al Coda
(take 1st ending)

— for you.

Gtr. 4

Gtr. 3

P.M.

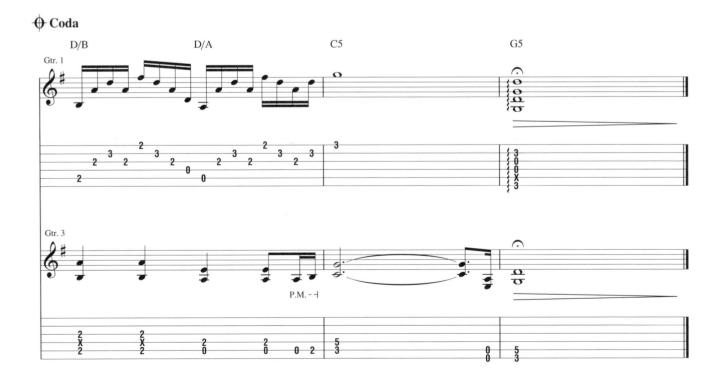

Coda

Gtr. 1

Gtr. 3

P.M.

Heretic

Words and Music by Matthew Sanders, Jonathan Seward, Brian Haner, Jr. and Zachary Baker

Drop D tuning:
(low to high) D-A-D-G-B-E

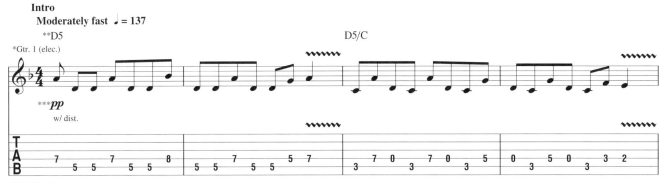

*Doubled throughout
**Chord symbols reflect implied harmony.
***Fade in (next 6 meas.)

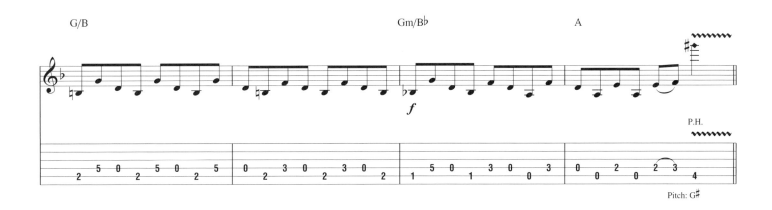

Pitch: G#

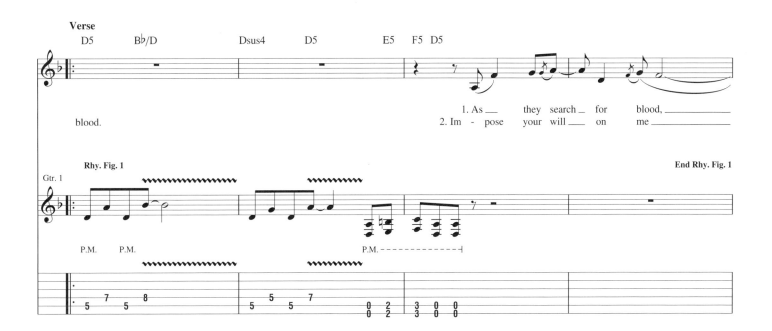

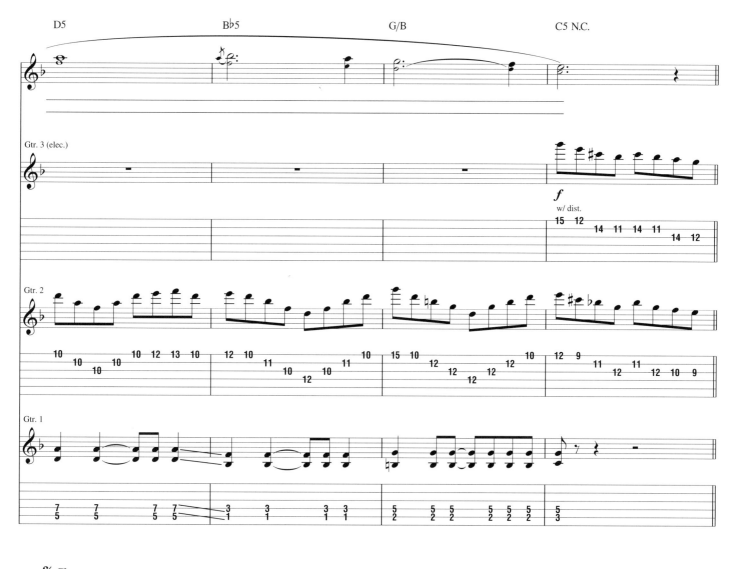

%: Chorus

3rd time, Gtrs. 2 & 3 tacet

Gtrs. 2 & 3 tacet

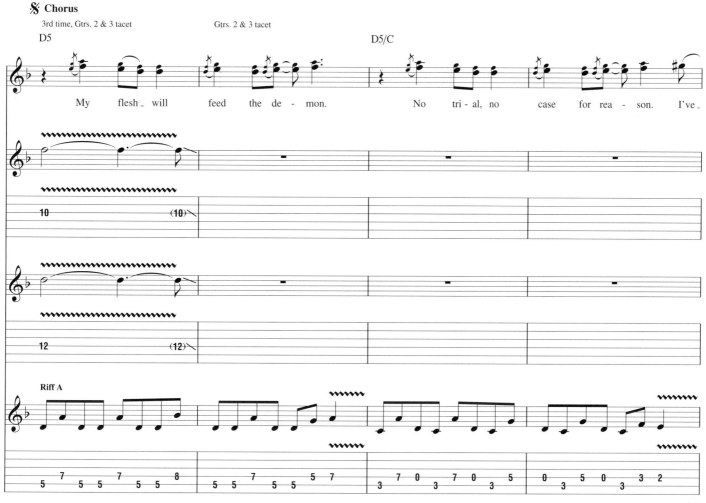

My flesh will feed the de - mon. No tri - al, no case for rea - son. I've

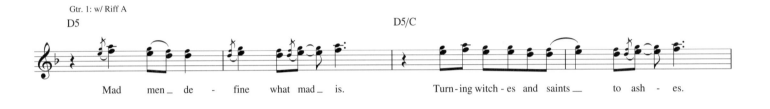

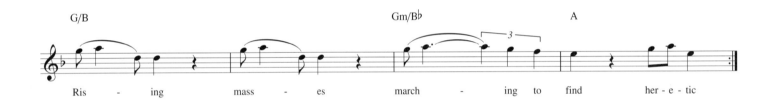

Interlude
Half-time feel

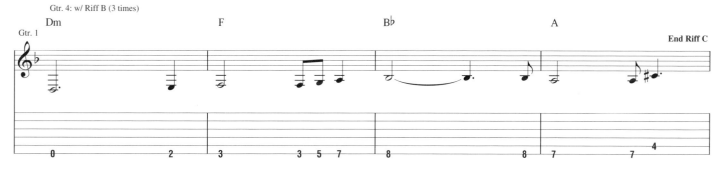

Please _____ don't __ leave __ me like this. __ I've

walked a frag - ile line _____ and I've fall - en _____ down. _____

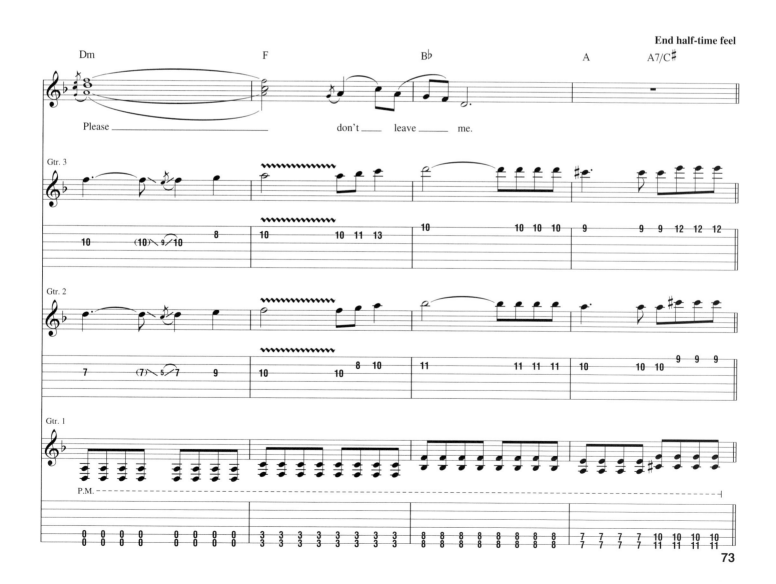

Please _____ don't __ leave __ me.

73

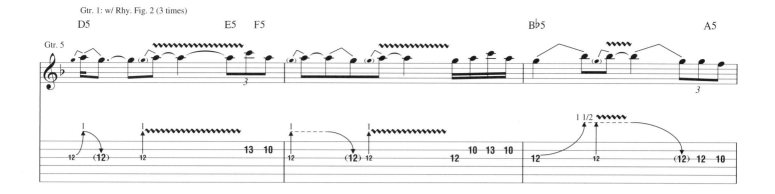

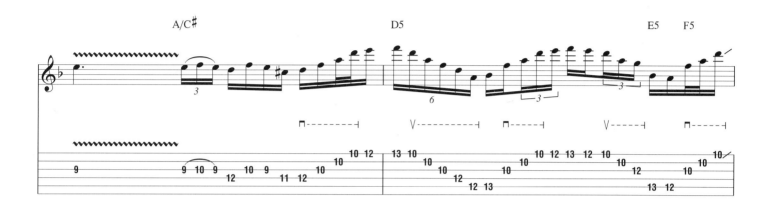

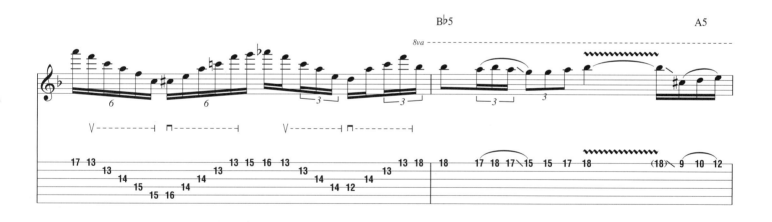

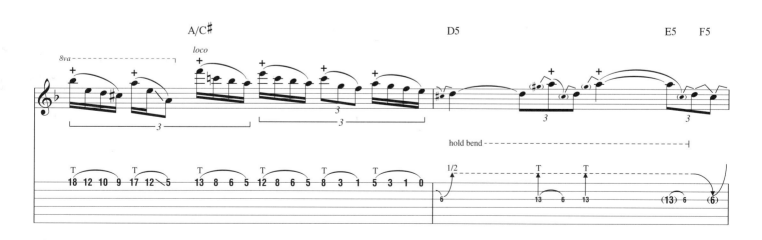

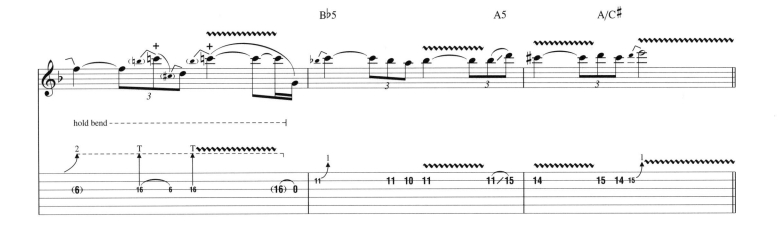

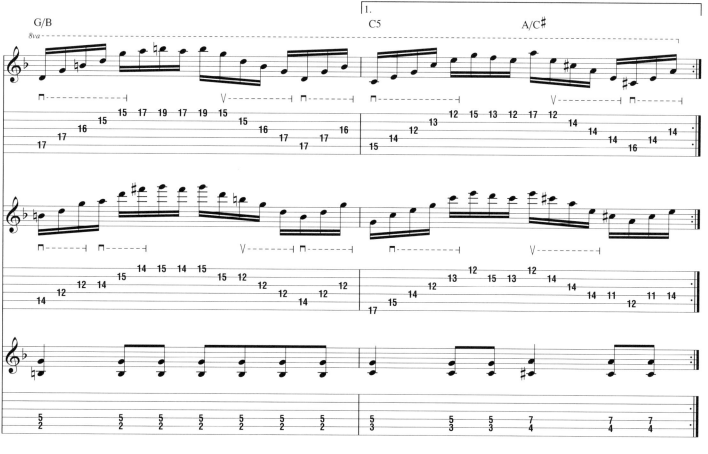

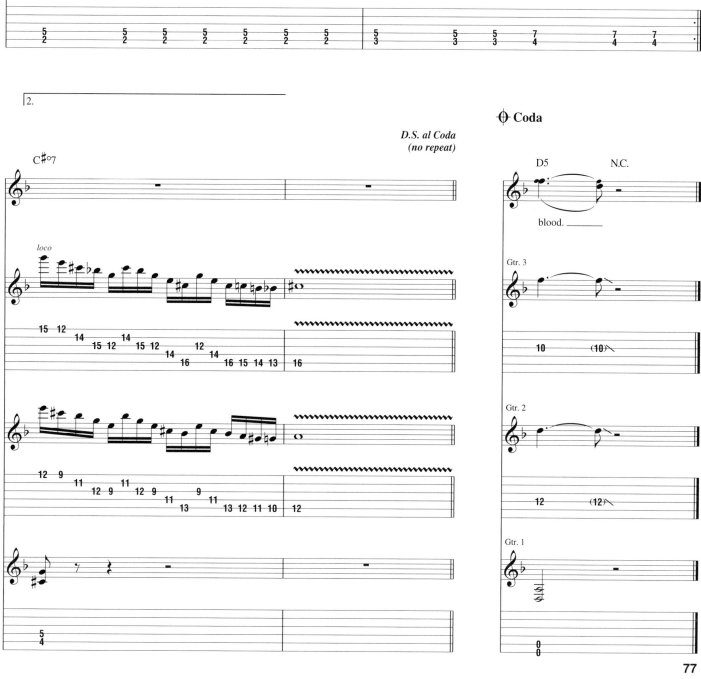

Coming Home

Words and Music by Matthew Sanders, Jonathan Seward, Brian Haner, Jr. and Zachary Baker

Drop D tuning, down 1/2 step:
(low to high) Db-Ab-Db-Gb-Bb-Eb

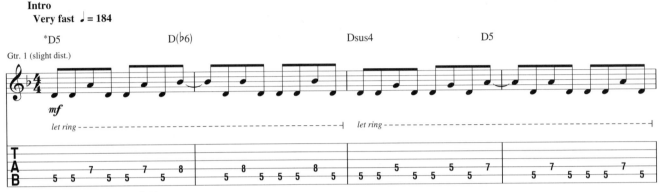

*Chord symbols reflect implied harmony.

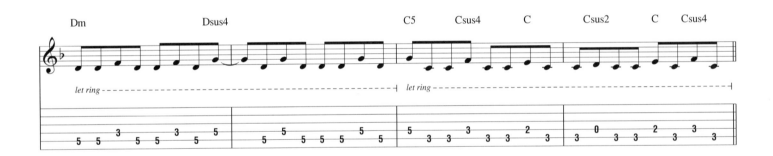

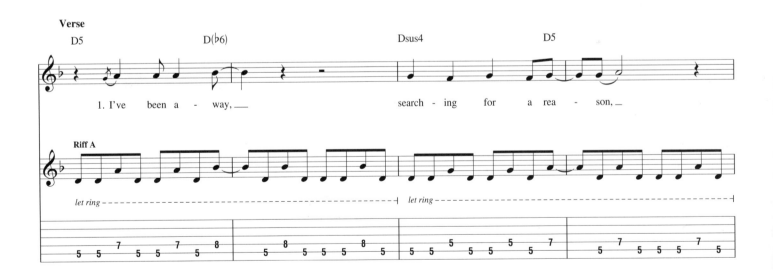

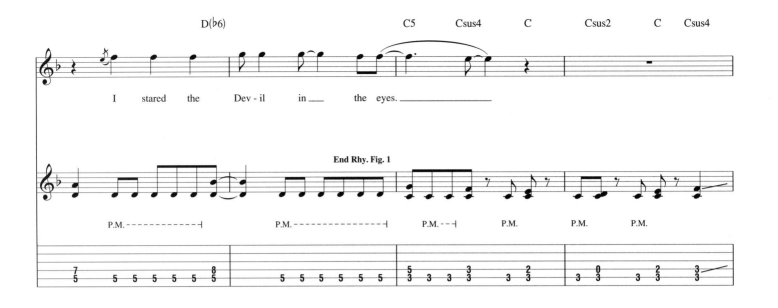

I stared the Dev-il in the eyes.

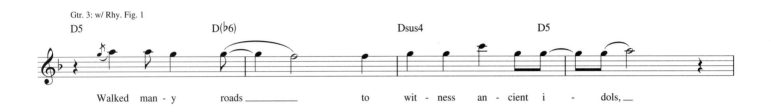

Gtr. 3: w/ Rhy. Fig. 1

Walked man-y roads to wit-ness an-cient i-dols,

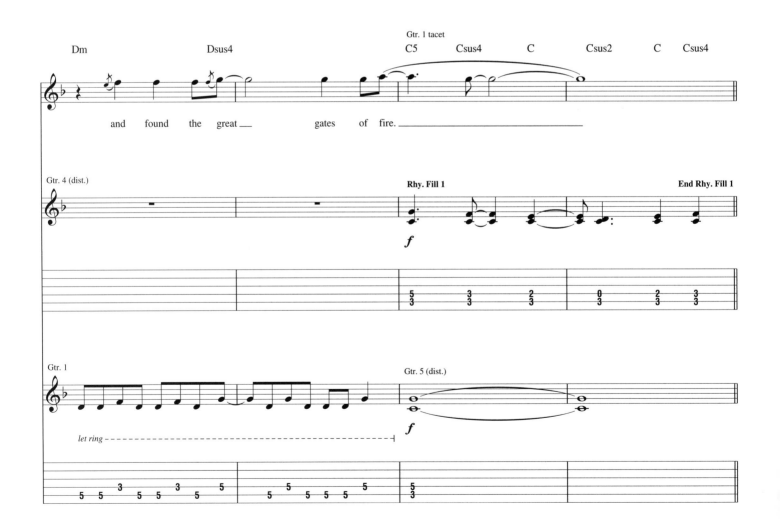

and found the great gates of fire.

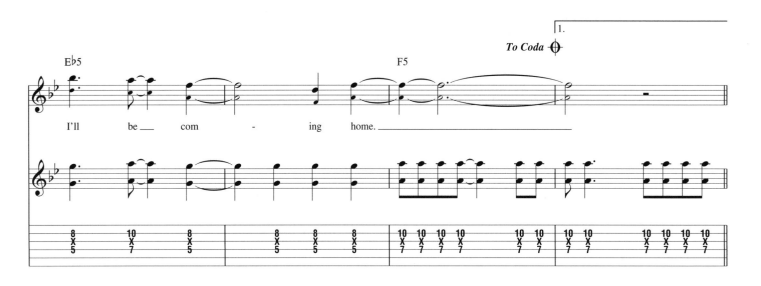

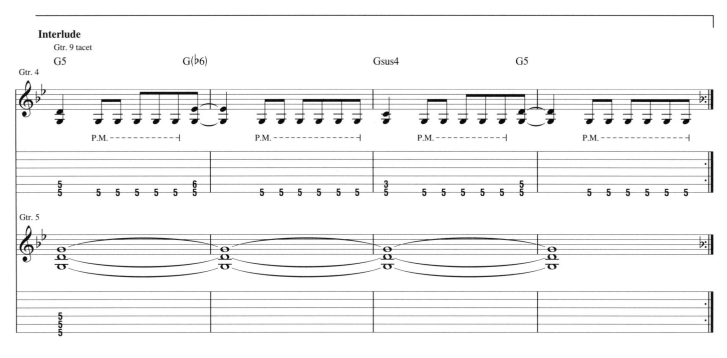

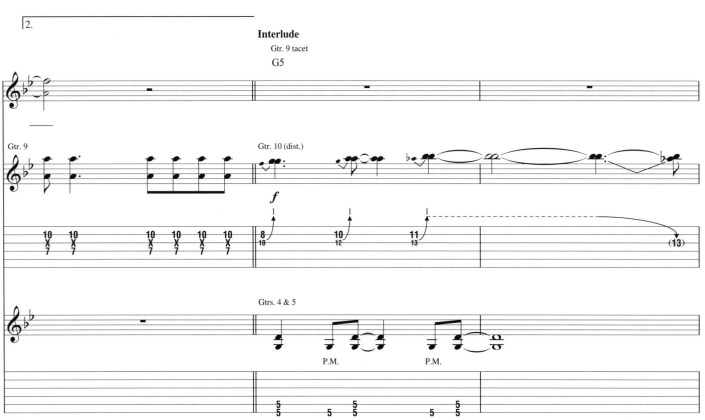

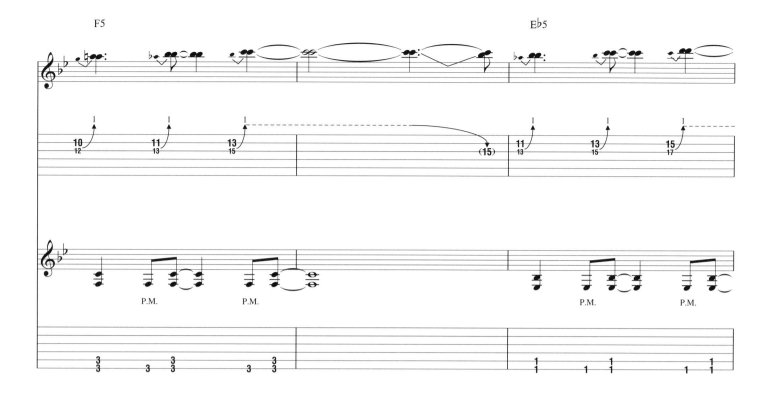

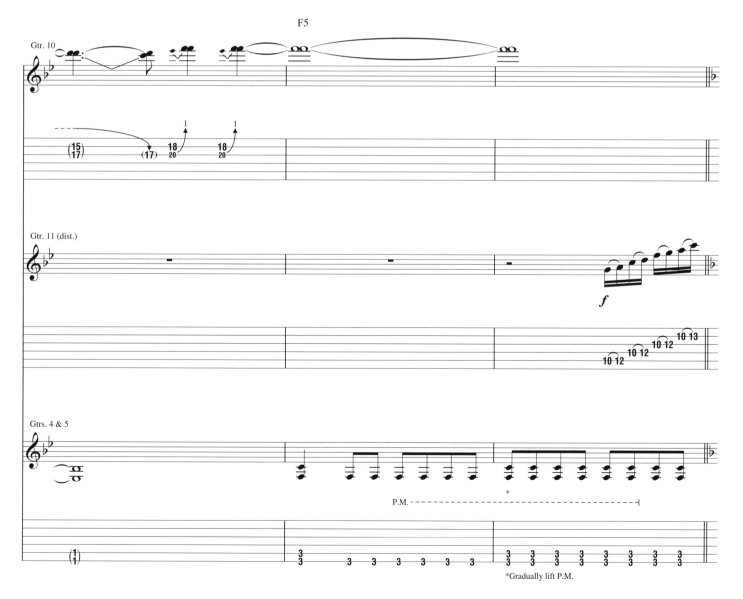

Guitar Solo

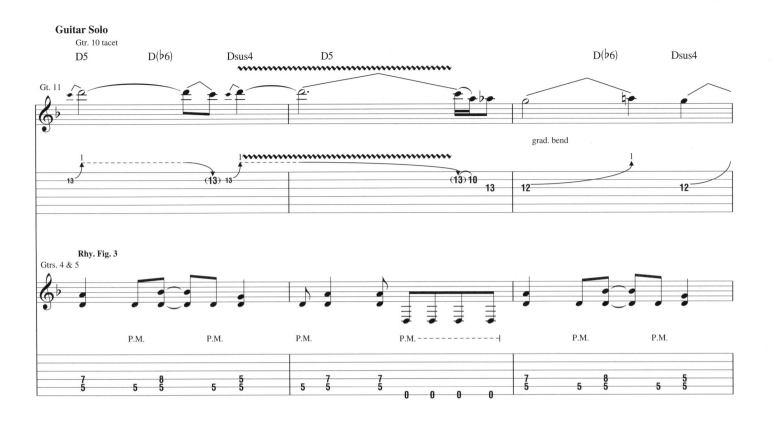

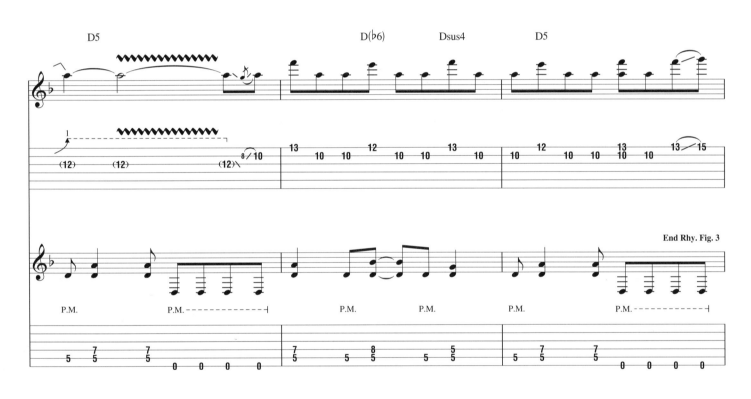

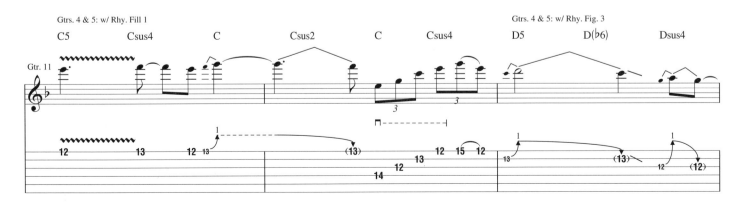

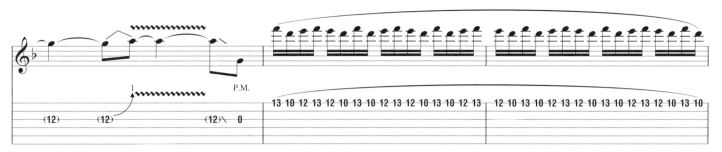
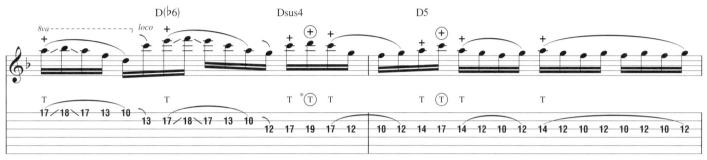

*Tap w/ ring finger.

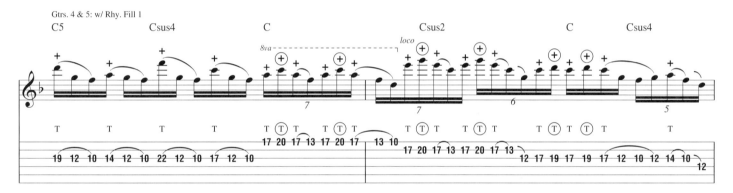

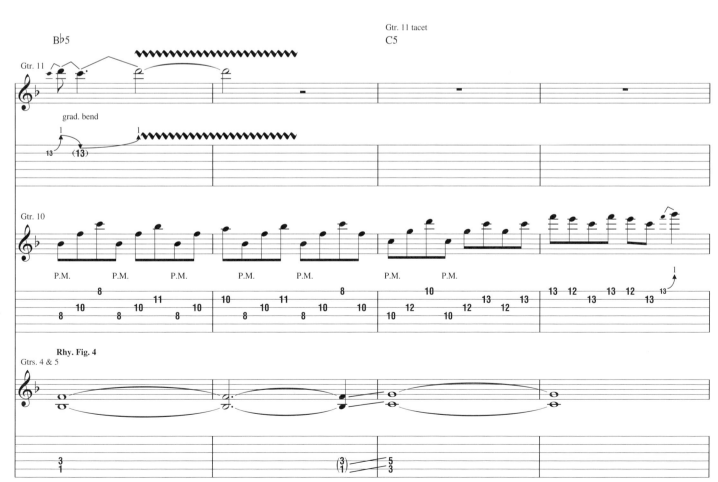

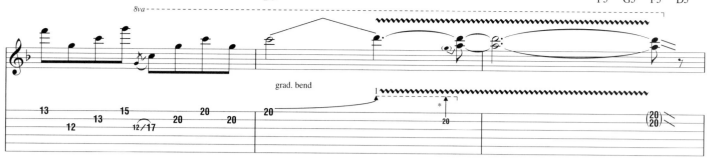

grad. bend

*2nd string caught w/ bend finger due to vib.; don't pick.

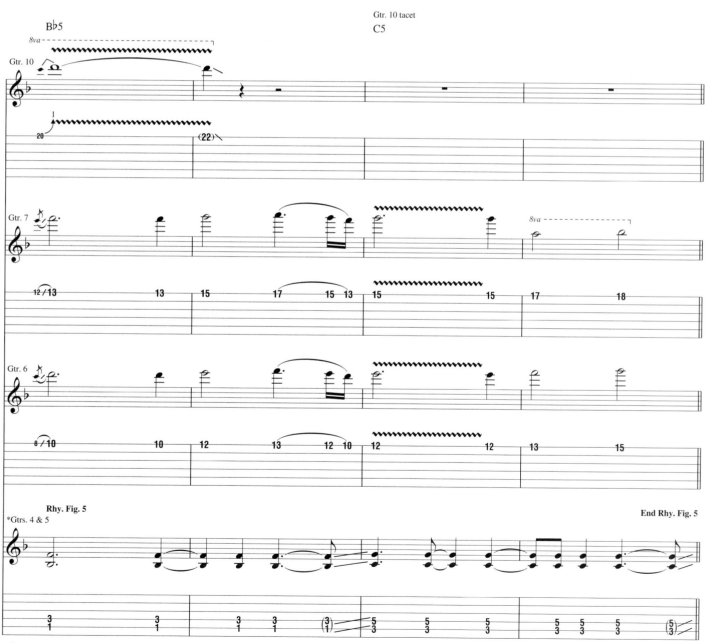

*Composite arrangement

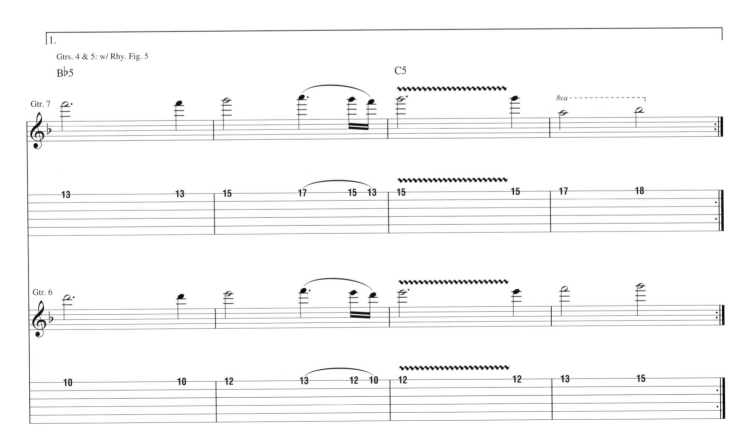

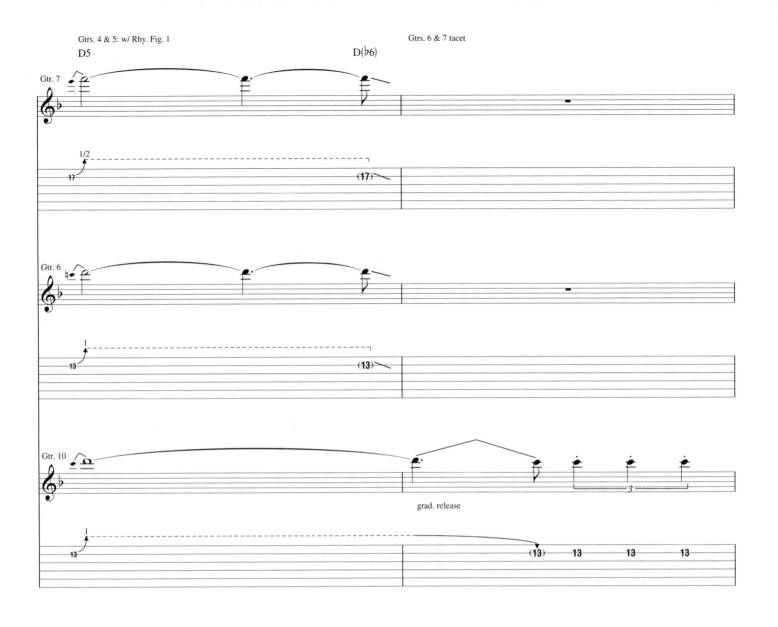

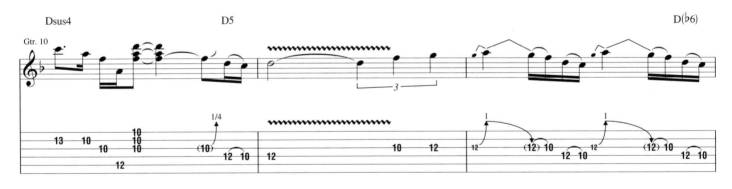

D.S. al Coda

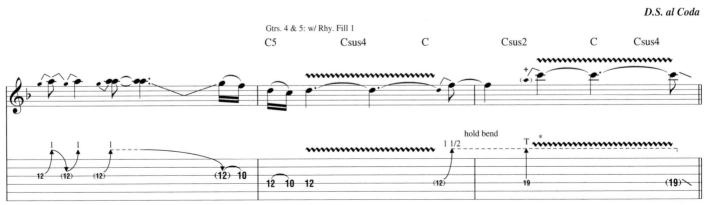

*Execute vib w/ frethand.

Coda

Outro-Guitar Solo

Gtrs. 4 & 5: w/ Rhy. Fig. 6 (till fade)
Gtrs. 6 & 7: w/ Riffs E & E1 (till fade)
Gtr. 9: w/ Riff D (till fade)

I'm _____ com - ing

Planets

Words and Music by Matthew Sanders, Jonathan Seward, Brian Haner, Jr. and Zachary Baker

Drop D tuning:
(low to high) D-A-D-G-B-E

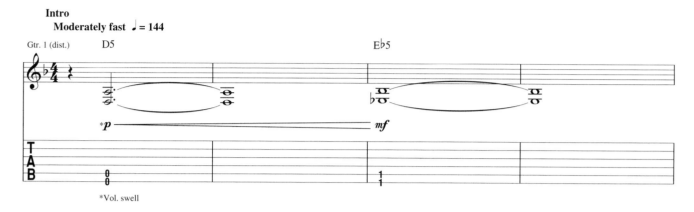

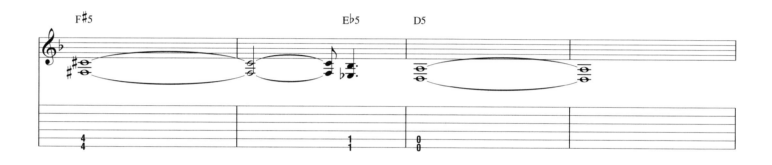

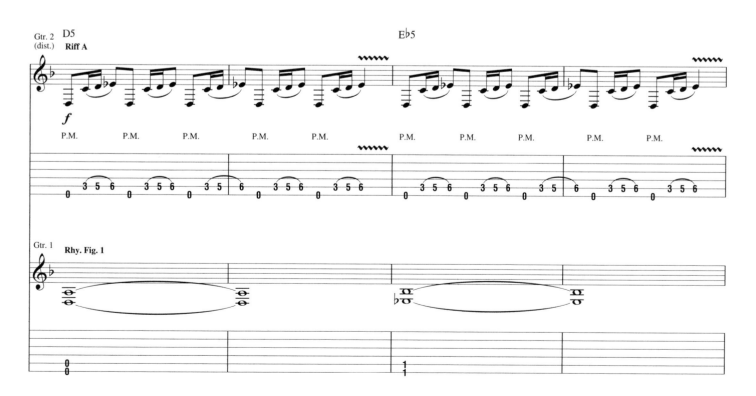

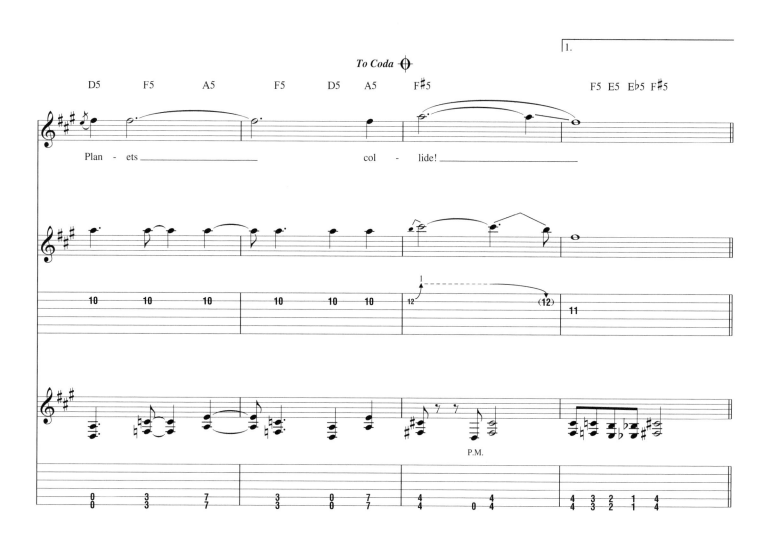

Interlude

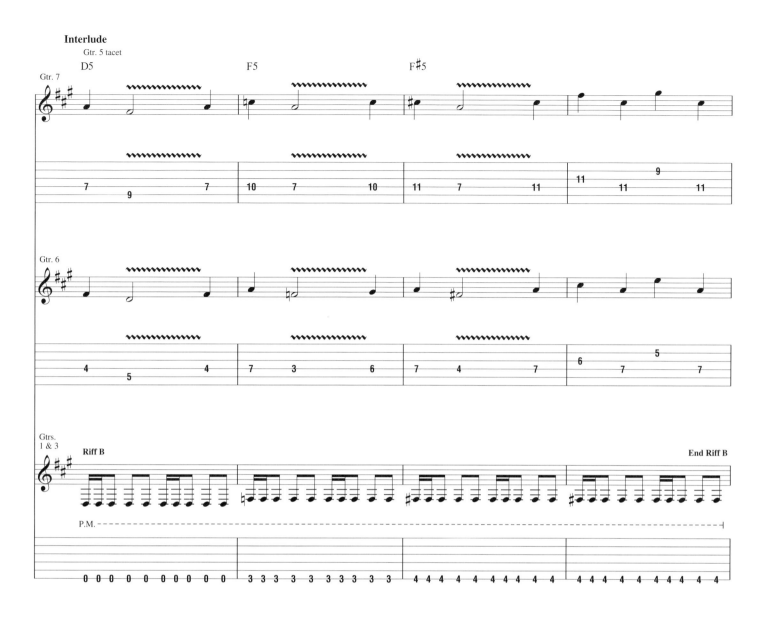

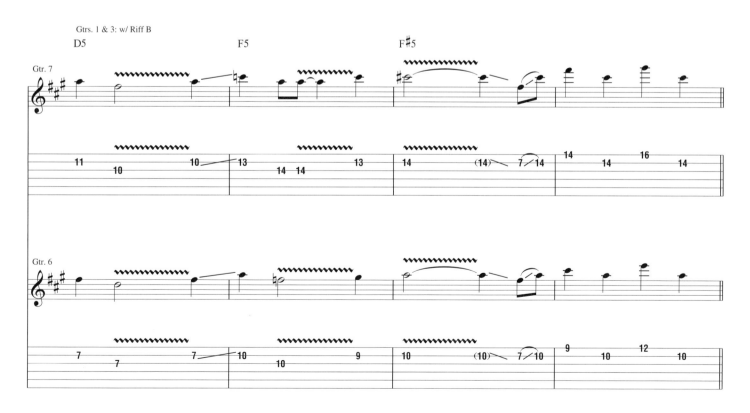

Bridge

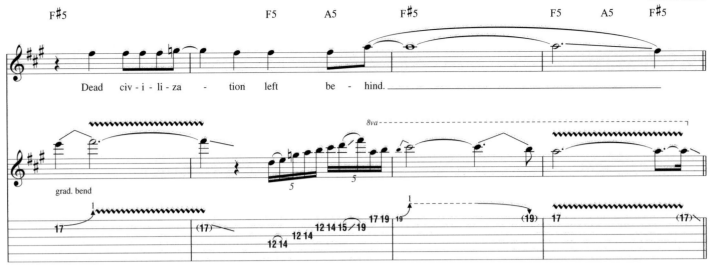

Dead civ-i-li-za-tion left be-hind.

Coda

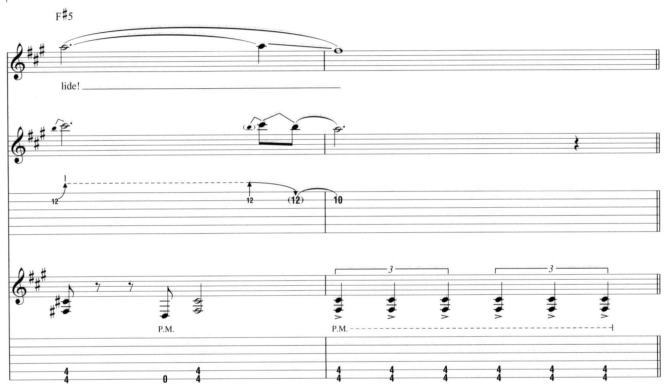

lide!

Outro-Guitar Solo
Half-time feel

Gtr. 5 tacet

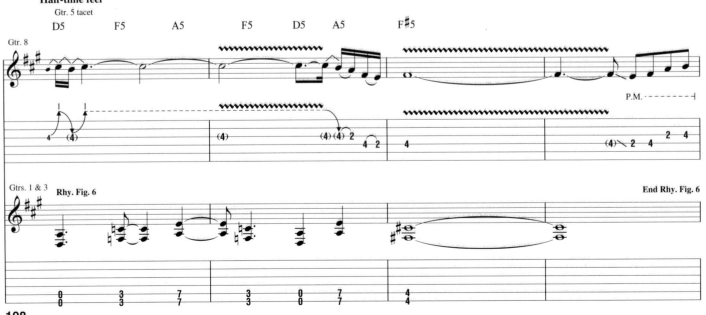

Gtrs. 1 & 3   Rhy. Fig. 6

End Rhy. Fig. 6

Acid Rain

Words and Music by Matthew Sanders, Jonathan Seward, Brian Haner, Jr. and Zachary Baker

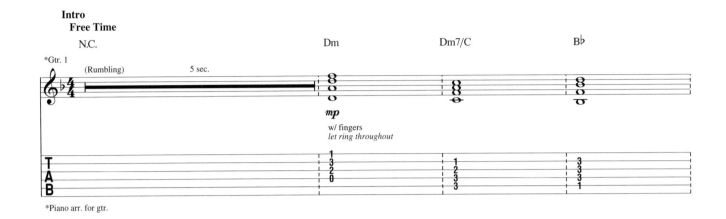

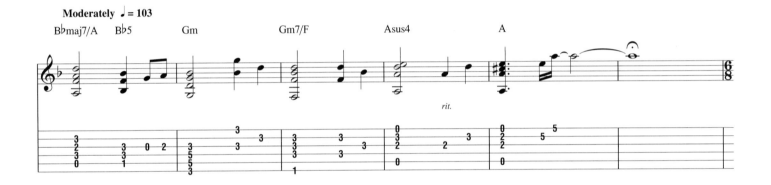

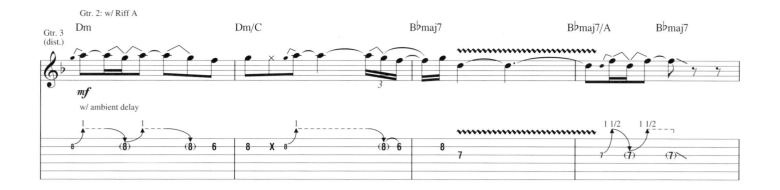

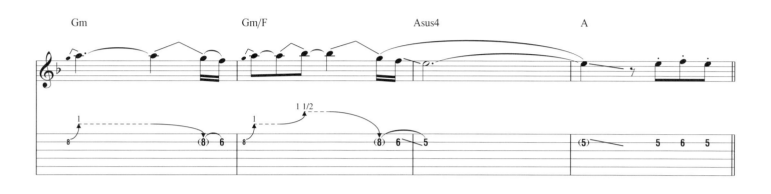

Verse

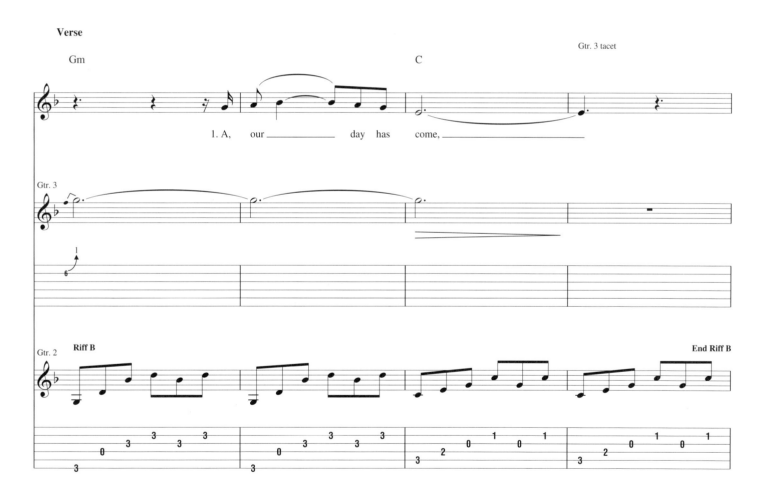

1. A, our _____ day has come, _____

Gtr. 3 tacet

Riff B

End Riff B

Gtr. 2: w/ Riff B (3 times)

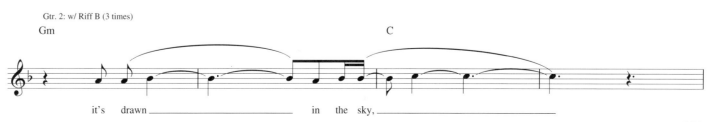

it's drawn _____ in the sky, _____

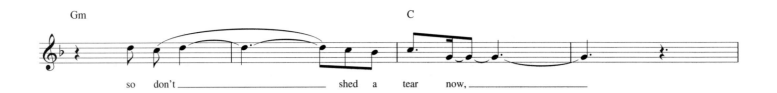

Gm   C

so don't   shed a tear now,

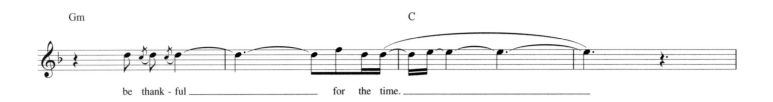

Gm   C

be thank - ful   for the time.

Pre-Chorus

A(♭9)

Life would-n't be so pre-cious, dear, __ if there nev-er was an end. _____

*Gtrs. 2 & 4 **Riff C**   ⌐3⌐   **End Riff C**

*Gtr. 4 (slight dist.), played *mf*.

Chorus

Gtrs. 2 & 4: w/ Riff A

Dm   Dm/C   B♭maj7   B♭maj7/A B♭maj7

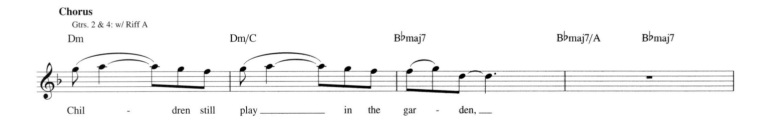

Chil - dren still play _____ in the gar - den, __

Gm   Gm/F   Asus4   A

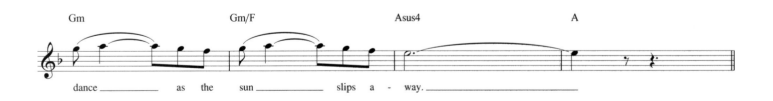

dance _____ as the sun _____ slips a - way. _____

Verse

Gtr. 2: w/ Riff B (4 times)

Gm   C

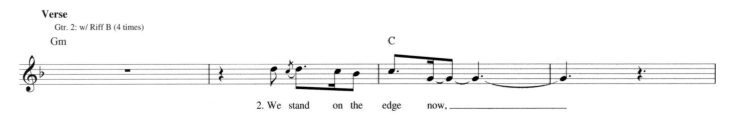

2. We stand on the edge now, _____

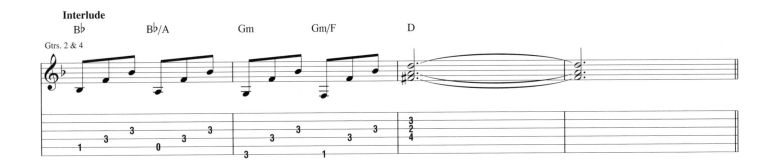

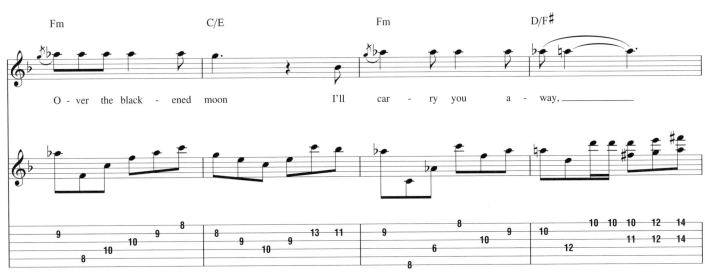

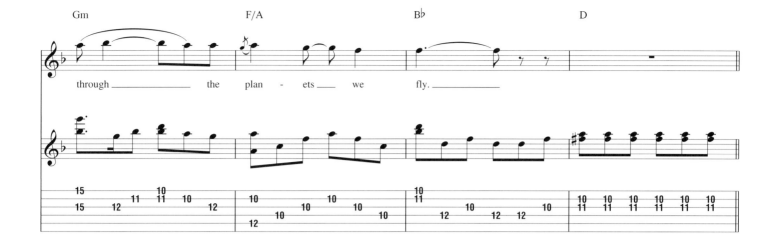

through _____ the plan - ets ____ we fly. _____

Guitar Solo
Gtr. 1 tacet
Gtr. 2: w/ Riff B (4 times)

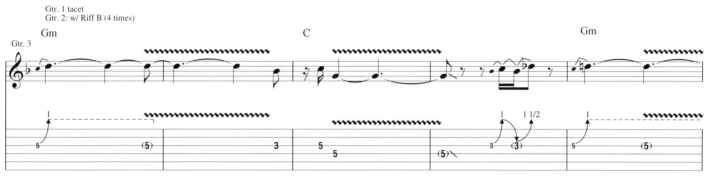

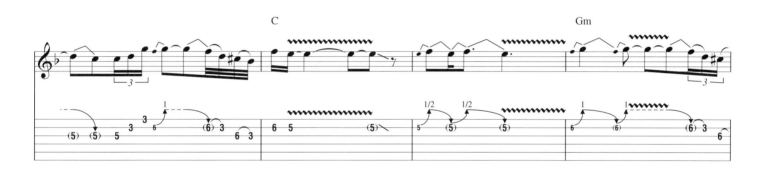

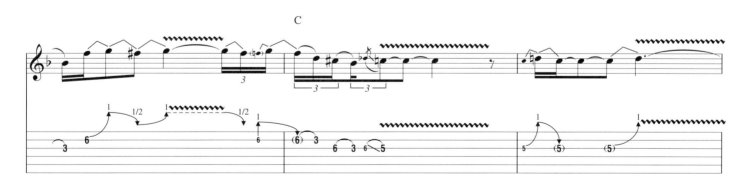

Gtrs. 2 & 4: w/ Riff C

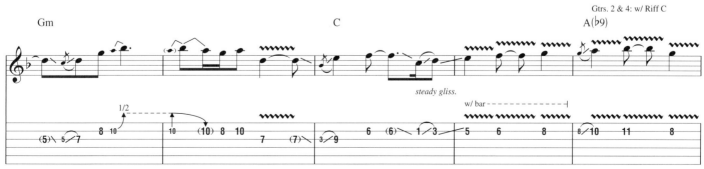

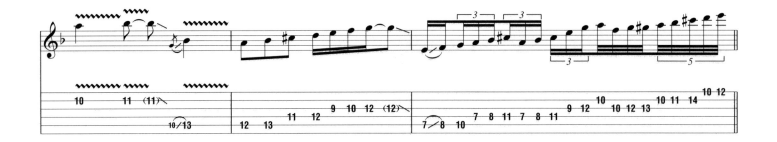

Chorus

Gtrs. 2 & 4: w/ Riff A (2 times)

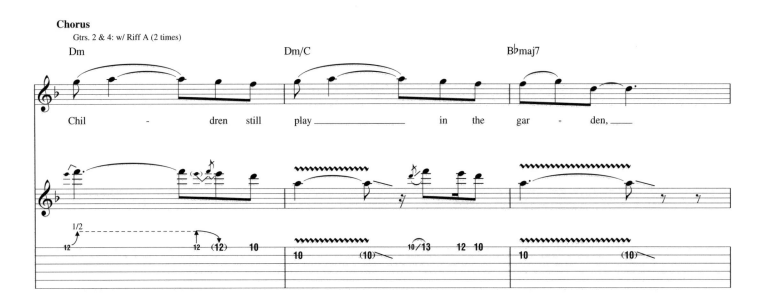

Chil - dren still play _____ in the gar - den, _____

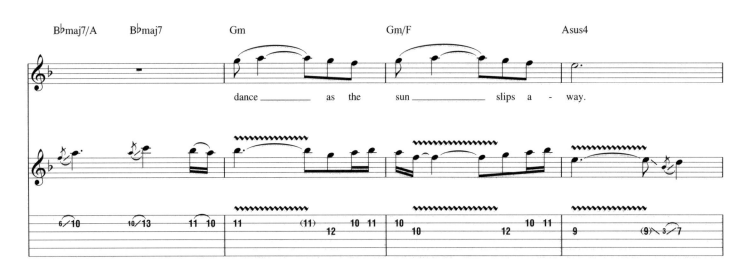

dance _____ as the sun _____ slips a - way.

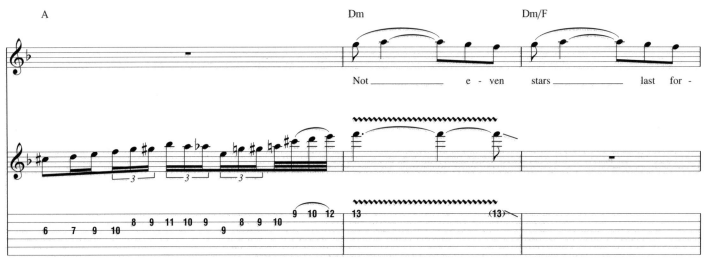

Not _____ e - ven stars _____ last for -

GUITAR NOTATION LEGEND

Guitar music can be notated three different ways: on a *musical staff*, in *tablature*, and in *rhythm slashes*.

RHYTHM SLASHES are written above the staff. Strum chords in the rhythm indicated. Use the chord diagrams found at the top of the first page of the transcription for the appropriate chord voicings. Round noteheads indicate single notes.

THE MUSICAL STAFF shows pitches and rhythms and is divided by bar lines into measures. Pitches are named after the first seven letters of the alphabet.

TABLATURE graphically represents the guitar fingerboard. Each horizontal line represents a string, and each number represents a fret.

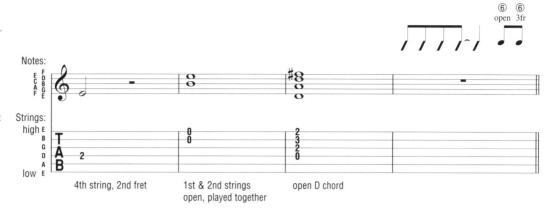

4th string, 2nd fret   1st & 2nd strings open, played together   open D chord

Definitions for Special Guitar Notation

HALF-STEP BEND: Strike the note and bend up 1/2 step.

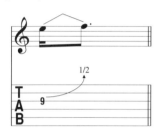

WHOLE-STEP BEND: Strike the note and bend up one step.

GRACE NOTE BEND: Strike the note and immediately bend up as indicated.

SLIGHT (MICROTONE) BEND: Strike the note and bend up 1/4 step.

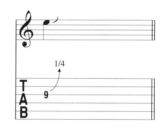

BEND AND RELEASE: Strike the note and bend up as indicated, then release back to the original note. Only the first note is struck.

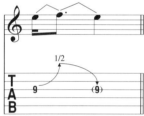
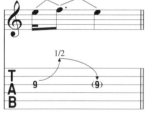

PRE-BEND: Bend the note as indicated, then strike it.

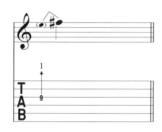

PRE-BEND AND RELEASE: Bend the note as indicated. Strike it and release the bend back to the original note.

UNISON BEND: Strike the two notes simultaneously and bend the lower note up to the pitch of the higher.

VIBRATO: The string is vibrated by rapidly bending and releasing the note with the fretting hand.

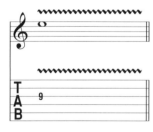

WIDE VIBRATO: The pitch is varied to a greater degree by vibrating with the fretting hand.

HAMMER-ON: Strike the first (lower) note with one finger, then sound the higher note (on the same string) with another finger by fretting it without picking.

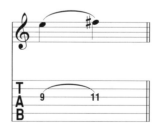

PULL-OFF: Place both fingers on the notes to be sounded. Strike the first note and without picking, pull the finger off to sound the second (lower) note.

LEGATO SLIDE: Strike the first note and then slide the same fret-hand finger up or down to the second note. The second note is not struck.

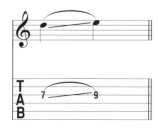

SHIFT SLIDE: Same as legato slide, except the second note is struck.

TRILL: Very rapidly alternate between the notes indicated by continuously hammering on and pulling off.

TAPPING: Hammer ("tap") the fret indicated with the pick-hand index or middle finger and pull off to the note fretted by the fret hand.

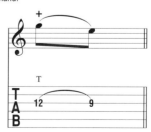

NATURAL HARMONIC: Strike the note while the fret-hand lightly touches the string directly over the fret indicated.

PINCH HARMONIC: The note is fretted normally and a harmonic is produced by adding the edge of the thumb or the tip of the index finger of the pick hand to the normal pick attack.

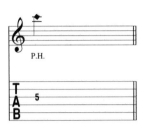

HARP HARMONIC: The note is fretted normally and a harmonic is produced by gently resting the pick hand's index finger directly above the indicated fret (in parentheses) while the pick hand's thumb or pick assists by plucking the appropriate string.

PICK SCRAPE: The edge of the pick is rubbed down (or up) the string, producing a scratchy sound.

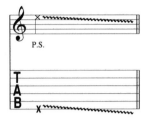

MUFFLED STRINGS: A percussive sound is produced by laying the fret hand across the string(s) without depressing, and striking them with the pick hand.

PALM MUTING: The note is partially muted by the pick hand lightly touching the string(s) just before the bridge.

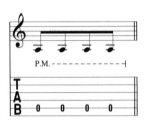

RAKE: Drag the pick across the strings indicated with a single motion.

TREMOLO PICKING: The note is picked as rapidly and continuously as possible.

ARPEGGIATE: Play the notes of the chord indicated by quickly rolling them from bottom to top.

VIBRATO BAR DIVE AND RETURN: The pitch of the note or chord is dropped a specified number of steps (in rhythm), then returned to the original pitch.

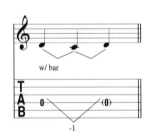

VIBRATO BAR SCOOP: Depress the bar just before striking the note, then quickly release the bar.

VIBRATO BAR DIP: Strike the note and then immediately drop a specified number of steps, then release back to the original pitch.

Additional Musical Definitions

(accent) • Accentuate note (play it louder).

(accent) • Accentuate note with great intensity.

(staccato) • Play the note short.

⊓ • Downstroke

V • Upstroke

D.S. al Coda • Go back to the sign (𝄉), then play until the measure marked "***To Coda***," then skip to the section labelled "**Coda**."

D.C. al Fine • Go back to the beginning of the song and play until the measure marked "***Fine***" (end).

Rhy. Fig. • Label used to recall a recurring accompaniment pattern (usually chordal).

Riff • Label used to recall composed, melodic lines (usually single notes) which recur.

Fill • Label used to identify a brief melodic figure which is to be inserted into the arrangement.

Rhy. Fill • A chordal version of a Fill.

tacet • Instrument is silent (drops out).

• Repeat measures between signs.

• When a repeated section has different endings, play the first ending only the first time and the second ending only the second time.

NOTE: Tablature numbers in parentheses mean:
1. The note is being sustained over a system (note in standard notation is tied), or
2. The note is sustained, but a new articulation (such as a hammer-on, pull-off, slide or vibrato) begins, or
3. The note is a barely audible "ghost" note (note in standard notation is also in parentheses).